Soft Gardens

Soft
Gardens

Make Flowers with Your Sewing Machine

Yvonne
Perez-Collins

CREATIVE MACHINE ARTS

CHILTON BOOK COMPANY

Radnor, Pennsylvania

Photography by Yvonne Perez-Collins
Illustrations by Jeanne Goullaud
Designed by Adrianne Onderdonk Dudden
Cover photos by Mark Jenkins
Cover design by Anthony Jacobson

Projects on the front and back cover were designed
by Yvonne Perez-Collins. The cacti on the back
were sewn by Mary Schaudies.

Manufactured in the United States of America

Library of Congress Cataloging-in-Publication Data

Perez-Collins, Yvonne.
    Soft gardens : make flowers with your sewing machine / Yvonne
Perez-Collins.
        p. cm. — (Creative machine arts)
    Includes bibliographical references and index.
    ISBN 0-8019-8327-4
    1. Fabric flowers. 2. Machine sewing. I. Title. II. Series:
Creative machine arts series.
TT890.5.P47   1993
745.594'3—dc20   92-28182
                                                         CIP

1 2 3 4 5 6 7 8 9 0   2 1 0 9 8 7 6 5 4 3

To Brittany and Kyle, who unknowingly took naps at all the right times so I could work on my soft gardens.

To my really great grandmothers, Ada, Nellie, Mary, and Phyllis, who have never stopped learning and sharing a passion for the sewing machine. You are my inspiration.

Thank you, Mom, for sewing all my clothes as I was growing up, for filling my life with flowers, and for quietly giving up your Bernina when I discovered it at a very young age.

Contents

Foreword

When you look through fashion and home decorating magazines, you can't ignore everyone's favorite accessory—flowers. I'm an inveterate clipper of magazine pictures and my flower file runneth over. I always thought that someday I'd use those ideas—somehow, somewhere. Then I read *Soft Gardens* and discovered that with Yvonne Perez-Collins' guidance, I could make any of the flowers I'd cut out of those magazine pages (and make each one in a dozen different ways).

Yvonne shows how to create fabric and thread appliqués and three-dimensional flowers using the latest products, tools, and her innovative how-tos. She gives us guidelines, but we can make our own choices. (As someone who loves originality, I'm in heaven.) She encourages those who are afraid to venture too far from packaged kits by telling them that even if they make mistakes, those mistakes can be turned into something wonderful. Then she goes on to save us hours of mistake-making by sharing the results of her own flower experiments.

Once we learn to make soft garden flowers, we're shown how to display them on hats, baskets, jewelry, corsages, vases, and fabric sacks—and in some cases we're shown how to make those, too.

Be prepared: After you read Yvonne's book, you'll be compelled to try all her ideas and file them (always in full view, of course) for when you need a gift or a decoration for your home or for yourself. I've always known that Yvonne Perez-Collins is a creative designer. After you read *Soft Gardens*, you'll know it, too.

Jackie Dodson
La Grange Park, Illinois

Preface

I like working with all types of fabrics, from industrial grades to designer silkies. I also enjoy all types of sewing machines—everything from a hand-crank model (used before electricity was invented) to a 32-head commercial embroidery machine. Sewing has been a very satisfying part of my life. In my sewing career I have made sails and accessories for boats and hang gliders, leather handbags and belts, and custom-fit pressure garments for burn victims. My own business of eight years started with making custom dome tents and bicycle clothing. Later, my company produced thousands of cycling caps and some appliquéd banners for athletic teams and businesses.

The appliqué work increased, and after taking classes, I found that doing creative stitchery on the sewing machine and teaching it were what I wanted to do.

Throughout this book I have suggested fabrics, supplies, and machine techniques for each project so you can have the same success and results that the photographs show. There are many other possibilities, however.

This book is devoted to those creative souls who deviate from instruction, as well as to those who follow instructions explicitly. Both types of artisans produce beautiful results. Once you realize which type you are, you can move on to more interesting results without apologizing when your work doesn't look anything like the teacher's, or when it looks exactly like everyone else's. If you enjoy the process of making it, you deserve the compliments. No apologies needed!

In my mind, there is a fine line between an artist creating with the use of unlimited supplies and an individual who is simply "making do" and puts a project together with supplies at home. Both are making decisions with what is available. There can be failure in either case, but there can certainly be success. There is a lot to be said for simplicity. You don't have to own a fabric store to make a fantastic creation—though we do our best to buy everything in the store.

I hope that you will enjoy the projects and techniques in this book. The next time you are going through your sewing stash or you're out shopping, try looking at textiles in a different way. Whether you see an old kimono in the closet or a bolt of tacky chiffon on the markdown table, think flowers.

Acknowledgments

Thanks to Pam Carroll, my first machine-embroidery teacher, who constantly reminded me that I was having fun as I struggled through the basic skills while breaking threads. You kept my feet on the ground until I was skilled and knowledgeable enough to be set free to create and challenge the rules.

Thanks to all the women and a few brave men who have been my students and my teachers. Aren't we lucky to have spent so many hours together having fun with the sewing machine?

Thanks to Debbie Casteel, who understands my need to create; to Bambi Stalder, who shares the need to create; and to Mary Osmus, who knew there was a book inside me trying to get out.

Especially, thanks to my husband, Roy, who gives me the chance to do what it takes to satisfy my appetite to create, get crazy, attend seminars out of town, make a huge mess, and skip the dishes when an idea is hot.

Soft Gardens

Introduction

This book is about creating fabric flowers. It shows how to use your sewing machine in different ways, to create and embellish fabric. I love the versatility and dependability of getting the same results every time I use the same setup on my machine. This is something that is harder to accomplish when I pick up a needle and stitch by hand. But part of me can't resist trying the same machine setup on different fabrics or with different threads as I let my ideas flow. Sometimes I feel like the medium from which they flow, like a psychic who communicates with another dimension. It's not that I have a great imagination, but, rather, a good vision. I use the materials I have at hand and apply them in different combinations.

I admire handwork, but I am usually interested more in knowing how the finished project was made than in the project itself. I often can devise a way to accomplish a similar effect using the sewing machine or serger.

Soft Gardens is aimed at three types of sewing enthusiasts: the quilter, the machine embroiderer, and the practical item/garment seamstress. We all gain immense satisfaction from using the sewing machine and collecting fabric, but usually we don't stray too far into other sewing realms. The projects in this book, however, will help you cross the line and let you wander around in my soft garden.

Soft Gardens features a well-rounded use of the various feet, tensions, and stitches on your sewing machine and introduces arts and crafts supplies that will complement your fabrics and threads. I hope it will open your mind to

other ideas that you might want to integrate with sewing projects.

For safety's sake, I provide technical information on such specialty tools as a soldering iron, as well as to pique your interest in the other possibilities of its use. Although the book covers the basics, I present many ideas so you can go beyond each project and use your imagination to create variations of your own. I like Aristotle's view on aesthetics "the unique realignment of alternatives." My own "aesthetics" sometimes happen after about ten accidents. That explains my machine stitchery, since I don't always stay inside the lines and am determined not to rip out stitches.

The methods used to create the flower petals and leaves and to assemble the flowers themselves are proposed in order of their simplicity. I suggest when to use the sewing machine whenever it offers you the right combination of the practical and the clever. Occasionally it will make better sense to stitch by hand or to glue. "The easy way out" is not the goal but a benefit of some techniques.

The book is set up as a reference of techniques. I suggest that you begin by reading the first three chapters. After that, choose the project that interests you. The other chapters cover appliqué, machine stitchery, three-dimensional pieces, flower centers, leaves and stems, display ideas, and vases and provide even more patterns.

Soft Gardens will give you the background to make fantasy flowers, as well as to imitate nature's work with the flowers in all stages of blooming. Make and give fabric flowers as a lasting reminder of a special occasion, a reminder that someone cares. A single flower can make a thoughtful impression when words alone are not enough. Flowers were made to cherish forever. Long after anyone can remember who made the flower or for what reason, it will still show the love and the time it took to make it. Handmade gifts may commemorate special times, like a significant birthday or anniversary. A new job can be greeted with English ivy in a coffee cup. A cactus dish garden would be the hit of a housewarming. A few scented flowers could be a nice addition to a new car.

1

Plant Your Ideas

Can we ever have too many flowers? A fresh bouquet certainly brightens the day, and in countless ways we can add their special touch with the help of the sewing machine. This and following chapters contain many possibilities, from appliqué to dimensional projects. Your choice of fabric, threads, and patterns will yield a beautiful variety of blooms from your soft garden.

Machine-embroidered and appliquéd flowers may look delicate, but actually they will withstand numerous washings on the garments they adorn. They will also add a special touch to towels, table linens, decorator pillows, and kitchen accessories.

Dimensional flowers have a particular charm, since they can be made using all types of fabrics—from everyday to designer textiles. The results are as subtle as a basket of wildflowers or as bold as a dazzling piece of jewelry. And what a benefit to find that these flowers are also easy to wash!

Follow the simple directions in this book to create your own soft garden of perennial blooms. Any of the dimensional flowers described can be attached to a stem and arranged in a vase. By constructing the flowers individually and adding a few leaves, you can fill a basket, pin a cluster on a hat, decorate a table runner, or top a gift box. Use one or more flowers to make your own corsage. Make sewn gifts even more special by adding a matching flower. Slippers, soft boxes, and travel cases offer a perfect background for a flower or two.

Before you take your first stitch, gather all the supplies you will need for your first project into a tray or basket. Start by matching all your fabrics, threads, and beads. Next, combine shades of those colors and a few contrasting colors as well. You probably won't have used all the supplies when your flowers are finished, but selecting the colors will start your creative juices flowing. I can't sit down and sew every time I want to, but gathering the supplies is a pleasant way to satisfy the immediate need to create. Seeing this colorful basket of supplies inspires me before and during the project.

Choosing Fabrics

Have you skipped ahead to the color pages? Are you ready to make a trip to the fabric store for a yard of this and a yard of that? Save yourself a trip and make samples with fabric you already have. Of course, the expensive silks and synthetic suedes will give fantastic results, but postpone the expense for a while until you experiment with flower sizes and shapes. Why not cut the lining out of a coat you're ready to give away or make bias strips from that out-of-fashion blouse? Do you have an old prom or bridesmaid's dress? Trust me: it feels good finally to get some use from S.O.s (space occupiers). Don't you have scraps from dresses that are begging to be made into a cabbage rose to match a new outfit?

Speaking of S.O.s, do you have any fabric you've made in classes in silk painting, tie-dy-

3

ing, batik, marbleizing, or screen printing? I've been hoarding my precious samples, but now is the time to turn them into something wonderful. All those experiments with applying color to fabric will come into full bloom. You will be so pleased with the results that you will probably take out all the supplies you used only once and do some more fabric painting and printing.

Once you have tried a pattern in one fabric, try some other fabrics for the same flower. Usually the lighter-weight fabrics give better results because they can be gathered easily. Heavier fabrics can work if you enlarge the pattern. Use a firm fabric to make giant flowers so the petals will hold their shape better. Try using the fabric on both the straight of grain and on the bias. The petals will either have crisp or soft folds, depending on the direction of the grain.

Many of the flower projects included here use woven fabrics, but be sure to try knits as well. Treat them as you would heavy, woven fabrics. Use them with larger patterns. The basic cabbage rose in Chapter 6 is made from a strip of fabric and is cut with the stretch going across the width of the strip. Some appliqué flowers may need tricot interfacing fused to the underside.

Suitable fabrics for appliqués or dimensional flowers and leaves include lace, velveteen, synthetic suede, moire taffeta, chiffon, prepleated nylon ruffling, Lycra, tissue lamé, bridal tulle, silk, tricot, lining, and crystal organza and nylon organdy. Choosing printed fabrics as well as solids will produce dramatic results.

Know Your Stabilizers

Before sewing any fabric flower to a fabric background and before doing any machine embroidery, you must decide if the fabric will need to be stabilized. Without a stabilizer, free-motion embroidery and even sewing with

a presser foot may be difficult. Even if you are diligent, your project still might pucker. Stabilizers will solve these problems and keep the sewing fun—as it should be.

Choosing the wrong stabilizer can compromise the outcome of your project. You may already have some stabilizers on hand, but others are worth looking for (see Supply Sources).

When sewing appliqués or decorating fabric with automatic machine stitches, use a simple stabilizer like plain white paper under the fabric or freezer paper pressed on the backside of the fabric. Keep in mind that these stabilizers will stay trapped in the stitching. If you are sewing long rows of stitching, 1"-wide (2.5cm) adding-machine tape makes a perfect stabilizer. Any time you remove paper from sewing, tear it toward the stitching so it doesn't pull out the stitches. Dampen the paper for easier tearing. It also helps to grip small pieces of paper with hemostats instead of your fingers. This handy tool can be found in medical supply stores.

Many commercial stabilizers are available in fabric stores and through mail order. Stitch-N-Tear, Tear-Away, and Totally Stable are three familiar brand names. You may find stabilizers in different weights (soft, stiff, crisp, iron-on), some with an iron-on backing and a newer kind in which the fibers that won't tear away will wash away. These tear-away stabilizers look just like nonwoven interfacings. Don't confuse the two, though, since interfacings will not stabilize machine stitching and cannot be torn away.

Perfect Sew is an exciting liquid fabric stabilizer from Palmer/Pletsch. Perfect Sew washes out and will stabilize even the sheerest and stretchiest fabrics. Seeing is believing. As the label says, it is the perfect solution for appliqué, buttonholes, machine embroidery, and heirloom sewing.

An easy way to apply the liquid is to work on a Formica counter or other nonporous work surface. Or place a Teflon pressing sheet under the fabric. Spread the stabilizer with a firm plastic spatula. Using a spatula minimizes waste, and the excess can be returned to the bottle. Clean all surfaces with water. You can speed up the initial drying of the liquid stabilizer with a hair dryer. When the fabric is slightly damp, complete the drying and remove the wrinkles by pressing with a warm, dry iron.

Always use a new needle so that you don't risk cutting the fibers. This rule is true for all sewing, but especially when the fabric has been treated with Perfect Sew. You will not need an embroidery hoop for appliqué. After you complete the stitching, remove the stabilizer by rinsing in warm running water or with a regular washing.

Another water-soluble stabilizer commonly used for machine embroidery is usually found where threads and other supplies for machine stitchery are sold (don't expect fabric stores to have it). Some of the product names are Aquasolv, Solvy, Wash-Away Plastic, and Hysilon. This film looks like the clear plastic used for dry cleaner's bags. It may be used to stabilize sweater knits, but it is primarily used for transferring embroidery patterns, then hooping the pattern on top of the fabric. Details are easily drawn on the water-soluble stabilizer instead of on the fabric. This also solves the problem of transferring a pattern onto dark-colored or textured fabrics like denim and terry cloth.

Other uses for this stabilizer are described in Chapter 4, when sewing a perfect satin stitch on appliqués and edges of petals; in Chapter 5, when making lacelike and solid-stitched flowers; in Chapter 7, when making tassel flower centers; and in Chapter 8, when making machine-stitched leaves.

Finding the right pen or pencil to draw patterns on water-soluble stabilizer successfully can be baffling. I have tried dozens of pens and pencils with only marginal results. Most

of them contain water-based inks. The permanent pigments can be thick, causing the sewing machine to skip stitches when sewing through it. After years of trying every kind of writing and drawing implement, I have found three that work superbly.

My first preference is Clotilde's washout pencil for dark fabrics. The soft lead can be sharpened to a fine point and writes easily on the stabilizer. The pencil is ideal for machine-embroidered laces because it will disappear when the stabilizer washes away. Sometimes the transfer pencil or pen marks become trapped in the embroidery stitching. Clotilde's embroidery tracing paper, made from the same substance, also works well.

Another good writing tool is the Pigma Micron .005 permanent marking pen by Sakura. The pens come in seven colors and six different point sizes, from superfine to bold. They write with the accuracy of a technical pen but without the hassle of refilling.

Sulky makes an iron-on transfer pen intended for fabric, but it also works well on water-soluble stabilizer. The pen comes in eight colors and works best on light-colored fabrics. I have seen a simple design drawn on paper with the black pen that transferred more than 40 times. Although I wouldn't have used some of the last transfers, I couldn't deny there was still a faint line. The other pen colors have varying ability in transferring up to ten times. Before ironing, layer as follows: paper towel, water-soluble stabilizer, transfer pattern (face down), paper towel. This way, the iron and ironing board are protected from direct contact with the stabilizer. Use a dry iron on a cotton setting and press firmly for ten seconds to transfer the design onto the water-soluble stabilizer. Let the paper cool before removing it so that the stabilizer will not become stretched and distorted. The edges may still curl but will relax after cooling. For reverse patterns, just turn the stabilizer over before stitching.

Threads Galore

I love thread. It is difficult to say whether I have more spools of thread or yards of fabric (Fig. 1.1). I select every spool carefully, and usually without a particular project in mind. Does that sound familiar? Threads vary in weight, texture, sheen, and twist. Using novelty threads or yarns in machine stitchery will highlight and enhance any project. For example, a bouquet of white flowers stitched with ten different white threads can be quite dramatic. You don't need every color of the rainbow to make a great creation, but it is fun collecting all the colors.

When you select colors for your projects and use thread on cardboard tubes, look at the thread on the end of the tube instead of where it winds around. This will give you a true reading of the color values, whether they are solid, ombré, or multicolored.

Machine-embroidery rayon thread is made in Germany, India, Mexico, Spain, and the United States. It is amazing how many colors I still don't have—even though my inventory is well over 500 spools. DMC cotton machine-embroidery thread comes from France.

Ombrés, multicolors, and metallics offer exciting embroidery possibilities. Madeira, a German manufacturer, boasts a wide variety and offers interesting threads made for machine stitchery, including wool blends, and 100 percent polyester for embroidery (the latter type holds up well in commercial laundering and bleaching).

Some threads are packaged in a cellophane wrapper. Always remove the wrapper because in time the ink used for the printing may damage the thread. Write the color number on the inside of the cardboard tube if the number appears only on the label. I also write the DMC embroidery cotton color numbers on the lip of the spool because in time the labels will become loose and fall off.

Many machine-stitchery enthusiasts wrap every spool of embroidery thread with thin plastic to keep moisture in the thread and to prevent it from raveling. They use the lightest-weight tablecloth vinyl, which sticks to itself and makes rubber bands or tape unnecessary. One day I discovered that the vinyls were leaching an oily film on the spools, so I dropped everything and removed every plastic wrapper. For some reason the plastic softens and breaks down. This chemical reaction occurred with every brand of thread, but it didn't seem to cause discoloration.

If you live in a dry climate and your thread breaks or shreds easily, place the thread in the refrigerator for a few hours to add moisture. Other solutions for problem threads are silicone lubricants called Sewer's Aid and Needle Lube (available in fabric stores). Squirting a line in two or three places along the length of the spool should keep brittle threads from breaking. Also try using a Schmetz #75 blue stretch needle to prevent shredding threads.

To secure thread on any kind of spool, tie a slipknot on the end and place the spool in the loop of the knot. Cinch it snug around the spool. You might have to break the thread the next time you want to free the end, but at

Fig. 1.1 Assorted rayon, metallic, cotton, and acrylic threads used for machine embroidery and traditional hand embroidery.

least the thread prevents the spool from un-raveling. For another knot that works well (although the procedure is difficult to explain), see Figure 1.2.

Nearly all the projects in this book will require using a bobbin filled with thread that matches the needle thread. The exceptions would be the appliqué projects in Chapter 4 and the Brazilian embroidery in Chapter 5. For this stitchery, I suggest using "regular" bobbin thread. Since machine embroidery is viewed only on the right side, it is customary to use a white cotton thread that is the same weight as the top thread. Sometimes called basting thread, it is made by Mettler, Zwicky, True-Sew, and Sew Bob. For good results, loosen the top tension slightly until the stitching on the wrong side shows $\frac{1}{3}$ bobbin thread and $\frac{2}{3}$ top thread.

As you acquire more bobbins filled with machine-embroidery thread, you will need an efficient way to store them. The rayon and metallic threads unwind easily and make a glorious mess. On a small piece of tape, fold one end under to make a tab. Tape the thread tail to the bobbin. Be sure to put the tape on the side of the bobbin that will face up when it is in the machine. This will prevent the sticky residue from causing problems in the bobbin case. Store your bobbins in a cough-drop box so they won't have room to roll around. One brand, Hold Cough Lozenges, comes in a clear plastic cylinder container that will hold seven bobbins. Put a cotton ball in the bottom so the first bobbin won't get stuck.

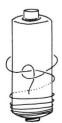

Fig. 1.2 Method of tying thread around a spool to prevent unwinding.

Monofilament is another useful thread and is used primarily in the needle. Because it is a fine thread, using it in the bobbin can risk a jam. Monofilament used for machine embroidery comes in clear, for light-color fabrics, and smoke, which is perfect for stitching on medium- to dark-colored fabrics. This thread has proven to be impervious to very hot irons and is used on quilts.

Over the years it seems that I have unintentionally started a collection of spool holders and thread guides for all kinds of slippery threads. These include everything from ones made by Elna and Bernina to the one I made by bending a bicycle spoke so the thread can pull up from the spool like it would on a serger. Some machine embroiderers have had satisfactory results by just placing the spool in a cup sitting on the table behind the sewing machine and then threading the machine normally. The search for the perfect spool holder stems from the ever-present dilemma of dealing with thread that is loosely wound on the cardboard tube. It just can't wait to jump off the spool and cause sewing machine tension nightmares.

I have had flawless results using a wooden spool holder with four dowels to accommodate all sizes of spools and bobbins (Fig. 1.3). The spool lies horizontally and the thread pulls off the side rather than off the end. This position still allows a slight tension so the thread won't pull off by itself. My husband made a spool holder from an exotic hardwood when he saw the crude version that I had been using for almost a year. I had pounded two 4" (10.2cm) nails in a block of wood that had a hole in the bottom so it could mount on the machine's thread spindle.

To make a simple spool holder, poke holes in the bottom of a 4" (10.2cm) block of foam rubber or Styrofoam for the vertical thread spindles on your sewing machine. Poke a pencil horizontally in the center front so only 4" (10.2cm) protrudes in front. Wrap a small

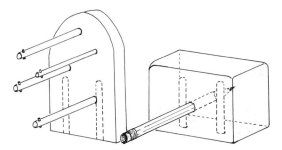

Fig. 1.3 Two examples of spool holders, (Left) One crafted in wood and (right) the other made from a block of Styrofoam and a pencil.

rubber band around the end to keep the spool from sliding off during sewing.

So many threads, so little time. A favorite thread mentioned in the Brazilian embroidery project in Chapter 5 is DMC pearl cotton, which comes in #3, #5, and #8 sizes, with #3 being the thickest. It is made in France and labeled as Perle cotton. The American generic name is pearl cotton.

Various hand-stitchery suppliers boast exciting threads. Some are too thick for threading through the machine needle, but they can be used in the bobbin beautifully or couched by stitching with monofilament on top. Kreinik Mfg. Co., Inc., makes metallic blending filaments, braids, ribbons, cable, and cord. Even its three glow-in-the-dark colors beg to be used in a fun project. Imagine the glow of satin-stitched petal edges.

Transfer Methods

Do you currently mark your fabric with dressmaker's carbon paper or a sliver of soap? If so, you will be pleased to know that there are many other successful ways to transfer patterns onto fabric. Most of the time you will want the transfer medium to wash away. Clotilde's washout pencil and transfer paper work as efficiently as the blue washout pens found

in fabric stores. Make sure that you don't iron over the areas marked with the blue pen and heat-set the ink. The purple or pink disappearing ink pens work best in dry climates. On humid or rainy days, the lines may disappear right away. You can keep your design safe by folding the fabric and storing it in a plastic bag until you are ready to use it.

Water-soluble graphite pencils used by quilters are available at art supply stores. The Swiss crayons that blend with water also wash away, but they are expensive and don't keep a point as well as the pencils made by the same manufacturer. These are not typical sewing notions, but they do work.

When your felt pens are no longer good for writing, they are ready for sewing projects. I keep a special set of felt pens in my sewing room that I use for tracing around templates and making pattern notations. Because the ink is so faint, no one else wants to use them! They leave enough of a line for my purposes and always wash away (since the set was inexpensive and therefore of cheap quality).

Permanent transfer mediums usually have been more destructive than helpful because they bleed into the fabric and permanently discolor the stitching long after the project is complete. In years past, permanent markers made thick lines that were difficult to cover and eventually bled into the fabric as well.

Technology has rewarded us with pens that work without a hitch. The Pigma Micron pen (discussed earlier in this chapter in the stabilizer section) makes superfine lines on fabric that are easily covered with stitching. When used for shading or vein lines in fabric flowers, the pigment will not fade like other permanent inks. Sakura also makes permanent fabric markers, called Fashion Craft, in 24 fashion colors. Before using fabric pens and paints, prewash the fabric to remove sizing, and, for best results, the fabric content should be at least 20 percent cotton. Cover the painted fabric with a clean cloth and heat-set with a very hot, dry iron. To prevent scorching, move the iron slowly.

Fabric markers are used to color the felt, batting, and thread stickers and blossoms in the Cactus Dish Garden in Chapter 6. Using the markers in this way enhances the color presentation of the cactus shapes. Color blending, in fact, is one of the more successful techniques using fabric markers. It is not possible to heat-set the color for the Cactus Dish Garden because it is three-dimensional.

One old and infamous transfer pencil had a maroon-colored lead that would leave pink lines on the fabric. Think twice before using this pencil on a project. A safer solution for drawing a pattern on paper and then pressing the design on fabric is to use Sulky's iron-on transfer pen. This pen works beautifully on every kind of fabric I have tried, including water-soluble stabilizer, lace, felt, sheers, and synthetic suedes in light to medium colors.

When using a dry iron on the cotton setting, press for up to ten seconds to transfer the image. This is long enough to render a good image without damaging the fabric. Press for only a few seconds if you want a lighter image. The ink is permanent, and the eight colors also can be used to transfer shading. This transfer method is ideal when you have

to cut out a variety of pattern shapes or a series of the same pattern shape.

To correct a transfer that has already been inked, use two coats of white correction fluid on the areas you wish to remove, or make the corrections on the paper. To save a pattern for future use, transfer one copy on paper. Whenever a transfer's image starts to fade, re-ink it so that you won't have to redraw it from scratch.

Sewing-Machine Stitches and Settings

Take inventory of all the stitches that your sewing machine can make. I classify stitches in four ways:

1 The functional stitches common to most sewing machines, including a blind hem, stretch blind hem, overedge, and stretch overedge.

2 The satin stitches, which have round, almond, diamond, or triangle patterns.

3 The open stitches, which are delicate and look like hand-stitchery patterns, such as the honeycomb and feather stitch.

4 The motif stitches, such as hearts, ducks, sailboats, or any other design.

Stitch Length	Stitches per 25mm (or 2.5cm or 1 inch)
.5mm	50
1.0mm	25
1.5mm	16-17
2.0mm	12-13
2.5mm	10
3.0mm	8
3.5mm	7
4.0mm	6
4.5mm	5-6
5.0mm	5
5.5mm	4-5
6.0mm	2-3

Don't feel limited by the stitches you have. They will multiply when you use them in combinations or when you use a double needle threaded with two colors of thread. The stitch pattern, by the way, will be almost unrecognizable when one of the threads is multicolored.

Chapter 2 describes how to set up for a perfect satin stitch and free-motion embroidery. The top thread and bobbin tensions are explained simply so that you can start on any project without having prior machine-embroidery experience. I suggest balanced tension for some projects, particularly when you want the stitch to look good on both sides of the fabric. When using a foot and when doing free-motion work, I suggest a stitch length. The conversion chart by Jeannie Horton (page 9) will help you understand the actual length of the stitch as it is indicated on your machine. Her article in *Treadleart* magazine (vol. 14, March–April 1992) explains the American use of inches converted to metric, as many sewing machine manufacturers have done.

Presser Feet and Accessories

Of all the feet and accessories that came with your sewing machine, do you use only the all-purpose foot, zipper foot, or appliqué foot? Have you made the daring choice yet to use the clear plastic foot? These fabric flower projects will take you by the hand and encourage you to use a few more attachments and feet to facilitate your sewing effort and really make the sewing fun (Fig. 1.4).

Most sewing machines come with a blind-hem foot. Look at the bottom of the foot and notice the bar that aligns the folded fabric when sewing a blind hem. Like the edge-stitching foot, this will guide your fabric shapes for smooth satin stitching on the edge.

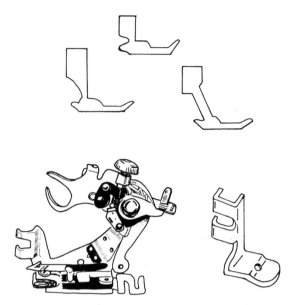

Fig. 1.4 (Top) Profiles of high, low, and slant shanks. Useful machine attachments: (left) ruffler and (right) gathering foot.

A ruffler is used in Chapter 4 to make a pleated rosette. This unique attachment is not that familiar to the average seamstress, but it works efficiently to stitch pleats in fabric or trim. *Learning and Using Your Ruffler* by Leota Black provides thorough technical information and a few projects (see the Bibliography). When sewing over wire for veins or edges, Chapter 8 suggests an assortment of specialty feet and explains how to use them. Use a gathering foot for the quick task of making strips of ruffled organdy for cactus edges and for gathering the edges of the Cabbage Rose in Chapter 6, and for making leaves in Chapter 8. The Crowning Touch makes a foot called Fastube that is used for sewing bias tubes for making the Nosegay of Loops in Chapter 6.

Sewing-machine stores usually have drawers or walls full of accessories for the brands of machines they sell. You might even have some attachments from past sewing machines that will work on your current machine. Sometimes a different foot will pop right onto the shank. Other times they need a little customizing. Before you ruin the shank, try the foot on an adapter that may fit many different brands of snap-on feet. For example, Clotilde carries a special adapter that allows a Bernina to use low-shank accessories.

If mail order is your main source of supplies, the Sewing Emporium Catalogue is your gold mine for sewing-machine attachments and adapters. The catalogue illustrates a full assortment and gives a detailed description of each foot and attachment and their uses. Clotilde's catalogue includes adapters and specialty feet for sewing pearls, sequins, and ribbon and for topstitching.

Once you have an adapter, you will enjoy the wide selection of attachments that will allow you to sew trims, edges, cording, elastic, and many other tasks. I enjoy using feet from all brands and ages of sewing machines. About the only limitation is that a low-shank machine cannot use high-shank feet. Also, the Singer slant shank is in a world of its own when it comes to attachments. No others will adapt. There is an important point to remember if you own a newer machine with a 7 to 9mm-wide stitch capability. You will need to customize other manufacturers' feet to accommodate the wide swing of the needle by making a wider opening for the needle.

If you are handy in the garage or can bribe a small project out of someone who is handy, you have a few more options when customizing feet. First, make sure the foot fits on your machine before you start making changes. Then you can take out the hacksaw, grinder, and epoxy. The left or right sides of the foot can be trimmed for edge stitching and for making piping. A small jump ring or section of a tube can be glued to the center top of an appliqué foot for couching yarn or cord.

How about making a customized foot that has better visibility than the darning foot but doesn't move up and down? This foot would be helpful with quilted fabrics because, believe it or not, the lower portion of the foot is cut off. Then only the long section of the shank remains to hold down the thick layers. It is also helpful with some sewing machines to minimize the bouncing of hooped fabrics during machine embroidery. After the foot has been cut, the bottom of it will be ⅛" from the machine's cover plate when the presser bar is down. If your machine has snap-on feet, you will see that the plain shank is too long when you lower the presser bar and will not allow the fabric to move freely. Sometimes all you need to do is lower the feed dogs. If you have an extra foot (it doesn't matter what kind), give this one a try.

Other Tools and Equipment

Although this book is about creating flowers on the sewing machine, I include helpful information for using a serger if it might complement your work. Chapter 3 explains how to accomplish a perfect rolled edge on your serger. To produce quality work, the home sewer needs tools and equipment that industry has used for decades. Now every sewing machine company has answered this demand by making many different models of sergers. The good news is that the companies are highly competitive and have made constant improvements to make operating a serger a breeze.

Pinking shears were an important sewing tool before machines had stretch and overcast stitches. When the serger was redesigned for home use, the avid seamstress rarely needed to use pinking shears. My earliest recollection of their use was on the edges of Mom's old photographs. If you still have some pinking shears in your sewing box, keep them handy for petal edges and for pinking edges in the Cactus Dish Garden in Chapter 6.

Another unusual shear, the scalloping shear,

cuts a delightful edge in two different styles of scallops. This shear, which can be used on the Cactus Dish Garden, the faux suede flowers, and on fabric-covered vases, is available through the Sewing Emporium catalogue. The wavy-edge shear made by Clover cuts an edge that ripples like a pinked edge but without the points. It provides an attractive alternative to the serrated edge. Both styles of shears can be used by left- and right-handed sewers. (See Figure 1.5 for examples of cutting patterns.)

A travel iron and ironing pad are handy for small sewing projects and will spare you from setting up your full-size ironing board. The smaller sole plate on the travel iron is convenient when you need to do only minimal pressing. I made an ironing pad from an empty cardboard bolt that I cut to fit in my sewing travel case (at 16" [40.5cm] long). The length of the bolt is the same width as an old hand towel that wraps around the bolt for padding. The cover is a piece of solid-color fabric whose selvage was fused on the length of one edge for a smooth finish. I folded the fabric on the short ends like the wrapping on a present and then hand-stitched it closed.

If you enjoy heirloom or French hand sewing, you are probably familiar with the puff iron. The base clamps on the edge of a table and the egg-shaped iron extends from a short rod. The puff iron is designed to solve the difficult problems of ironing ruffles, puffed sleeves, and children's clothes. Fabric flowers

and leaves and bows can be pressed over the oval before and after assembling them.

For some projects, you will need a basic 15- or 30-watt soldering iron. Electronics stores carry many inexpensive models. Some irons come with only one tip, while others include an assortment. Select a tip that most resembles a needle or a sharpened pencil. Most of the cutting you will do will be done with the last ¼" (6mm) of the tip. Always follow all manufacturer's instructions when using a soldering iron.

There are other uses for a soldering iron, and a similar, 100-watt iron, used for leading stained glass and other big jobs, sells for $20 to $45. Sailmakers also use this iron as a "hot needle" to pierce and tack two pieces of nylon sailcloth together instead of using straight pins. The tip of the iron is surrounded by a spring that assists in making an accurate pinhole. Quilters and toll painters use a soldering iron with a fine tip to cut custom-designed stencils from a sheet of stencil plastic, and leather workers use one to burn patterns in the leather. Finally, wood sculptors use this tool to burn textures and patterns that resemble fur or feathers on wooden decoys or figures.

If you have a sewing room, you probably have a cutting table. The height of the table is a personal choice that depends on how tall you are and the kind of work you will be doing. When designing my cutting table, I kept these points in mind:

1 I want to be able to reach across the table as far as possible to smooth fabrics, make marks, take measurements, and cut and design patterns.

2 Since I will use the table for serging, occasional ironing on a pad, and glue-gun projects, I need room for my legs when seated on a stool and want electrical outlets nearby.

3 Rolls of fabric are stored above the table, so I need to stand on the table safely to

Fig. 1.5 Cut edges made with specialty shears: pinking, wavy-edge and two using scalloping shears.

reach them. Unlike most sewing tables, mine is sturdy, specifically designed and built so that I *can* stand on it.

4 I need a surface to accommodate design work and to use a rotary cutter.

5 I always need more storage space!

My 30"-high (.8m) cutting table suits all my needs (see Fig. 1.6.) The top is 4' × 7' (1.2m × 1.8m), made to fit in the room. The surface is ¾" (19mm) particle board that has been primed and then sanded lightly (because the paint raises the grain). I painted it with two coats of off-white semigloss paint. This smooth surface will not snag fabrics and is perfect for design work, when I use pushpins to hold paper and fabric in place. It is also a great cutting surface for the rotary cutter, and it doesn't damage the blade. The hairline cuts in the table are barely visible.

I framed the table with maple to match the cabinets and I added a two-drawer file underneath the left end. The drawers have heavy-duty fully extending slides because they are 24" (61cm) deep and, as predicted, are filled to capacity. My husband, the builder, followed through with his motto, "If in doubt, build it stout." The table hasn't creaked a single time when I have stood on it.

My source of electricity comes from a hanging outlet to the right, within arm's reach and over the table so it doesn't whack anyone on the head. My husband and I hard-wired the end of a heavy-duty extension cord to a junction box in the ceiling. The 2' (61cm) cord is connected to the junction box with a strain relief. The hanging outlet allows the power cord to move freely while I work and helps prevent accidents. I appreciate the convenience and safety when using a commercial cloth cutter, soldering iron, glue gun, iron, engraving tool, or steamer. An overhead fluorescent light replaces the standard ceiling incandescent light fixture.

There are three shelves above the cutting

Fig. 1.6 The cutting table in my sewing room with tools, storage, and hanging outlet incorporated for maximum use of space.

table that are 20", 25", and 30" deep, with the widest one at the top. This variance allows me to reach across the table without interference with the shelves and keeps the room from getting claustrophobic. The pegboard economizes wall space to display frequently used tools.

Underneath the table are neat rows and stacks of banker's boxes filled with fabric and supplies. The 30" (.8m) table height leaves ample space for stacking boxes two high and three deep. All boxes are numbered, and I keep a notebook listing the contents of each box. For my projects, it is easier to organize the fabrics by type rather than by color. The box of trims contains several gallon-size re-sealable plastic bags, used to sort elastics, bindings, tapes, and ribbons. Boxes of stabilizers, Ultrasuede, and laces are sorted the same way. To locate a particular box by moving as few boxes as possible, I refer to a grid that represents the stacking order of every box with a number. The system works like valet parking.

Unusual Sources

Fabric and craft stores will satisfy most of your needs in making most fabric flowers. I have researched all types of sewing and art supplies to find what is available to make these projects more fun, interesting, and easy to create.

You may share my fascination for using all types of novelty yarns, threads, and cords. If you limit yourself to only what fabric or machine-embroidery suppliers stock, you will have a great color selection, but the texture won't be too interesting. If you intend to do handwork, check cross-stitch, needlepoint, and needlepunch shops for unusual supplies. The yarns and cords may seem expensive, but a touch of texture around the edge of the petals or couched on vein lines will set your work apart from others, and actually you won't use much thread. You may also find beads, bells, and dingles to attach with machine stitching. I have made some of my best discoveries in hand-stitchery shops. If you can't run the thread through a machine needle, try using it in the bobbin or couching it down with monofilament threaded in the needle.

Leather-working suppliers offer tools that cut or punch holes in fabric. They can help you select the correct mallet and pounding surface. Although these tools would work best on synthetic suedes, you can punch holes in other fabrics, too.

Floral suppliers may seem to be the obvious choice to fill your needs when making fabric flowers. Let me remind you of the items to consider for your checklist. Most important: cloth-covered wire for stems and veins. Chapter 8 details wire gauges and their uses. You can choose from an endless variety of stamens for your flowers. Look for battery-operated lights, silk flowers, hats, baskets, wreaths, and vase possibilities. A floral-supply shop is also your best and possibly only source for wired-edge ribbon, also called French or silk ribbon, even though it is now made in the United States and is synthetic. Wired-edge ribbon is used for the Ribbon Flowers in Chapter 4.

Beyond these stores are sources for supplies that are not even remotely related to sewing or crafts. Medical supply stores are one such source. There you will find bent-nose locking tweezers and hemostats, both of which are good for removing stabilizers from machine stitching. Hemostats can be used to clamp onto a batch of stuffing and place it accurately and release it easily. You already may have discovered that the paper on the doctor's examining table makes great pattern paper.

Woodworking stores sometimes carry supplies for the toy maker. Wooden candle cups and bean-pot cups can be used for the calyx on some fabric flowers, as in the Nosegay of Loops project in Chapter 6. They also can be used to fasten the flower to a wooden dowel stem. Other wooden shapes can be combined to make unusual vases.

Now for a tour of the electronics store. You will find soldering irons and accessories and even locking tweezers with parallel blades for holding seed beads while stitching them using a sewing machine. Don't forget that the soft, fine wire for petal edges is called "wire-wrapping wire."

Plastics stores sell Plexiglas, Mylar, acetate, and other synthetic materials for commercial use. They also carry two items I couldn't do without: Teflon sheets and inexpensive plastic for making templates. You will be surprised at the range of thicknesses in which Teflon sheets are available. Most sewing sources sell a lightweight prepackaged pressing sheet. I find that the 5-mil sheet is sturdier and easier to work with because it won't wrinkle like the lighter sheet.

These suppliers carry a plastic called H.I.S. (high-impact styrene) that comes in various thicknesses and is perfect for permanent patterns and templates. A 15-mil sheet is firm but still light enough for cutting with scissors. The white sheets are transparent enough to allow tracing. I often splice pattern pieces with packing tape acting as hinges so they can be folded for easy storage. H.I.S. templates are more durable than cardboard because the corners stay sharp and won't disintegrate when you use a felt pen for tracing.

2

Basic Machine Techniques

For a lesson in the most current techniques of machine embroidery as well as supplies, sit back, relax, and read this chapter whether you are new to machine embroidery or already accomplished. You will find tips on making minor adjustments to your sewing machine, such as changing the top tension, that will improve the quality of your regular sewing, too. If manipulating your machine makes you nervous, just remember that the more you learn, the better your sewing will be.

Before getting into the creative part of appliquéd flowers, read the following information about how to work with almost any kind of fabric used for the background. Whether decorating a garment or home furnishing, the background fabric for fabric flowers will be either knit or woven.

Sewing on Wovens

Appliqués often are finished with a satin stitch using an embroidery or appliqué foot. This foot has a wide groove on the underside for the stitching to pass smoothly. An "open-toe" appliqúe foot has an opening in the center for better visibility (Fig. 2.4). This method may sound simple, but let's take a few additional steps to ensure a smooth, professional finish without puckers. In addition to proper machine tension, consider using a hoop or stabilizer.

Lighter-weight background fabrics require using a hoop or stabilizer because they tend to pucker easily, while heavier background fabrics are more stable and need little help.

Refer to Chapter 1 for detailed information on various stabilizers and how to use them. Some stabilizers can be hooped with the background fabric, or, when this isn't possible, the stabilizer can be pinned in place until the stitching can hold it.

I almost always use a wooden hoop when embroidering on lighter-weight woven fabrics (Fig. 2.1). The high-quality wooden hoops made in Germany are narrow, with sturdy hardware, including a slotted screw. (See Threads in the Supply Sources.) These hoops are made especially for machine embroidery and can easily be inserted into the machine.

Fig. 2.1 Wooden and spring hoops used for machine embroidery.

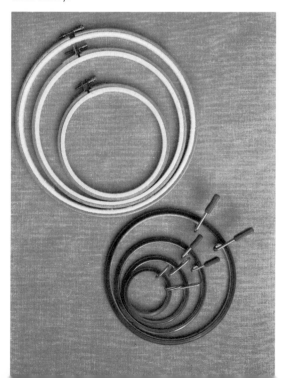

Inexpensive craft hoops are difficult to use on a sewing machine because the fabric loosens in the hoop during stitching. The fabric needs to be stretched taut so it will not slip while you are sewing. A 6" to 8" (152mm to 203mm) hoop is ideal for a sewing machine.

Here are some recommendations on wooden hoop preparation by Joy Clucas, from England. Many times the ends on the outer ring of wooden hoops curve slightly towards the inner ring. They should be sanded lightly so the inner ring makes an even contact with the outer ring. To facilitate stretching fabrics, lightly sand the inner ring on its outer edges. This slight curve allows the inner ring to pop into position more easily during hooping. To lessen the possibility of the fabric slipping out of tension, wrap the inner ring with twill tape or ½" Stay Tape (used to stabilize seams in knits). Secure the end by hand-stitching it on top or inside the inner ring.

I prefer to use spring hoops when working with medium to heavy woven fabrics. Because these fabrics are firm, they don't need to be stretched into wooden hoops. Just pop them into a spring hoop. A 5" (127mm) hoop fits comfortably in your hands and permits smooth movement for controlled stitching. A 7" (178mm) hoop will accommodate a larger embroidery area but will be more difficult to maneuver within the open arm of the sewing machine. The inner, metal ring of 5" and 7" spring hoops can be wrapped with ½" wide rayon medical tape (Dermicel) to minimize fabric loosening in the hoop. The tape is adhesive-backed, so rub a talcum powder on the wrapped hoop to absorb the excessive stickiness.

Consider using 2" (51mm), 3" (76mm), or 4" (102mm) spring hoops when an area on a garment would be difficult to fit into a larger hoop. Sometimes tricky areas on necklines and shoulder seams require a smaller hoop. The smaller the hoop, the better the tension on the fabric.

If a garment or a heavy fabric cannot be hooped, I stabilize it with freezer paper. This is a longtime favorite of machine-appliqué enthusiasts. Freezer paper tears away easily from satin stitching. since it will stay trapped in the stitching, freezer paper is not an appropriate stabilizer for delicate embroidery. Reynold's plastic-coated freezer paper will bond when pressed onto fabric. Cut a piece of freezer paper slightly larger than the embroidery pattern. Using a dry iron set on medium heat, press the plastic-coated side of the freezer paper to the wrong side of the fabric. The paper adheres easily and can be pressed again if it comes loose during stitching. Use an appliqué or darning foot to hold the work flat while stitching. If you have an area that doesn't tear away easily, make a perforated line by stitching around the embroidery without any thread in the needle or in the bobbin.

Sewing on Knits

You will enjoy wearing fabric flowers and embroidery on your favorite sweaters. The flowers are gorgeous and the stitching is easy. The right combination of hoop and backing will keep the knit stable. The following preparation for sewing is suitable for single and double knits, interlock, sweatshirt fleece, and sweater knits. The amount of stretch or stitch size in the knit will not limit the kind of machine stitching you can do as long as you stabilize the knit properly.

No matter what kind of knit you are working on, a spring hoop is better than a wooden hoop. Do-Sew and Trace-A-Pattern are lightweight pattern webs made of 100 percent polyester and are my choice of stabilizer for all knits. Some sewers prefer to use water-soluble film or paper-like tearaways for a stabilizer. I have used wooden hoops with these stabilizers on knits but find them difficult in comparison. Sometimes these stabilizers are mistaken for fusible webs when they are care-lessly stashed away unmarked in your sewing box. Always cut these two stabilizers large enough to cover the pattern area of the fabric to be hooped. When the embroidery is com-plete, trim the excess stabilizer to ¼" (6mm) from the stitching. This fabric is sheer and will soften with washing. The stabilizer accom-plishes a tremendous task with little effort.

Freezer paper is a suitable stabilizer for sweatshirt fabric when you are doing appliqué or solid stitching. Using a hoop isn't neces-sary. You may want to cut the sweatshirt open at the side seams, then reseam after finishing the embroidery.

Free-Motion Running Stitch

Free-motion embroidery allows the movement of hooped or stabilized fabric in any direction while stitching. This helps you attain greater creativity and freedom with your sewing ma-chine. Begin by removing the presser foot, shank, and screw. Lower the feed dogs. (Some machines have small snap-on covers that go over the feed dogs that cannot be lowered.) You may use a darning foot, darning spring, spring needle, or no attachment at all to assist the free-motion embroidery (these feet are de-scribed below, pages 20 to 21). A running stitch is a "straight stitch" using a 0 length/0 width that may curve, circle, sketch, or roam anywhere on the fabric that you desire. The stitch flows from the needle like ink from a pen.

Machine Setup

Stitch length: 0
Stitch width: 0
Feed dogs: down or covered
Presser foot: none, darning foot, or spring needle
Upper tension: looser than normal
Lower tension: normal

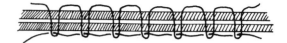

Fig. 2.2 Correct thread tension for machine embroi-dery when the top thread pulls to the wrong side of the fabric.

Needle size: #70 (10)–#80 (12)
Top thread: machine embroidery
Bobbin thread: regular
Hoop: 5"–7" (127mm–178mm) wooden or spring

The fabric should be hooped and possibly stabilized to prevent the finished stitching from puckering. I will suggest a stabilizer for each flower as needed. (Chapter 1 describes the stabilizers that can be used for creating fabric flowers.)

I once learned that if you remember whose fingers are holding your work, you won't let them get too close to the needle. Stitching without a presser foot will give you the best visibility while stitching. For most machine embroidery, this is the perfect setup. Some-times you will need to sacrifice visibility and use some sort of foot to help make the stitch-ing go more smoothly. Initially, you will have more professional results by using one of the accessory feet described in this chapter.

Generally, the bobbin tension should be tighter than normal for the running stitch. Otherwise the bobbin thread tends to pull to the top side of the fabric. This adjustment will correct that. The top tension for all machine embroidery is a little looser than normal. On the wrong side of the fabric, you should see both threads for every stitch (Fig. 2.2).

Methods for a Perfect Satin Stitch

Perhaps the most common and obvious solu-tion to the problem of how to finish the edge

A flower cart of "fresh stitched" flowers from soft gardens.

Sweater with English Loom Flowers by Bambi Stalder of Penngrove, California.

"Herein Is Love" jacket with dimensional velvet roses by Virgie Fisher of Sacramento, California.

Brittany Marie Collins wearing a garland of Suede Minis.

Straw hat with petals edged with fish line and centers made with a fringe foot. The leaves were made with the circle-leaf technique.

English Ivy made of suede
cloth.

Machine-Stitched Leaf Spray
with topaz Austrian crystal ber-
ries.

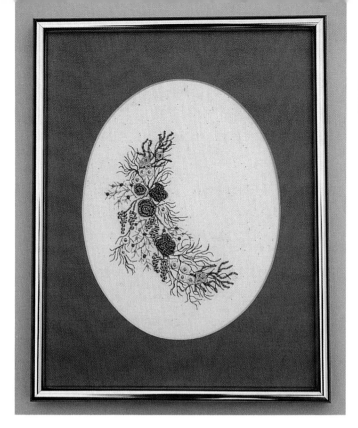

Brazilian embroidery made by Bette Bland of San Diego, California, with a sewing machine.

Ribbon roses with machine-stitched calyxes using an assortment of ribbons.

A daisy and poinsettia embroidered with shading and shaped to a free-flowing dimension to be worn as lapel pins.

Arrangement of flowers with two styles of petals in graduated sizes. The calyxes are circles of velour with pinked edges. Padded cachepot by Kitty Wan of San Diego, California.

Cactus Dish Garden with LED lights in the gravel, constructed with felt and single-knit fabrics by Mary Schaudies of Harlingen, Texas.

of an appliqué is to use a satin stitch. For that reason, I want to give you instructions on how to obtain perfect results.

Machine Setup

Stitch length: 0 (½ to ¼ if using an appliqué foot)
Stitch width: 2–4
Upper tension: looser than normal
Lower tension: normal
Feed dogs: up if using a foot
Presser foot: appliqué foot optional
Needle size: #70 (10)–#80 (12)
Top thread: machine embroidery
Bobbin thread: regular
Hoop: 5"–7" (127mm–178mm) spring or wooden

The satin stitch is a zigzag stitch with a very short length. Set the machine for a 0 length if you are using a darning spring, darning foot, spring needle, or no foot at all, since the length will be determined by how fast you move the work. If you use an appliqué foot, the length will range from ½ to ¼ since all machines will vary slightly. The top tension is slightly looser than normal and the bobbin is normal to a little tighter. Perfect tension for a satin stitch will show ⅓ bobbin thread and ⅔ top thread on the wrong side of the fabric (Fig. 2.3).

A satin stitch should be only as wide as the appliqué pattern allows. A 3 width usually is sufficient. For banners or large projects, consider a wider stitch for strength and aesthetics. For stitching around small shapes, don't use anything narrower than a 2 width. No matter what width you choose, the goal is for the

greatest part of the satin stitch to cover the edge of the appliqué, which prevents the appliqué fabric from pulling out. Before I satin stitch, I press a fusible web to the wrong side of the piece to be appliquéd and then press it on the background fabric. This process is described in detail in Chapter 3. (See Chapter 1 for stabilizers and later in this chapter for edge treatments to use with a satin stitch.)

If short fabric threads poke out through the satin stitch, you might want to run a second pass of satin stitching. It is better to stitch a sample first and ensure good results with one pass of stitching instead of relying on a second stitching to clean it up. A second pass works only when you are able to go over the original stitching using a wider width and can stitch with precision to cover the edge exactly as you did the first time. A second pass on rolled or lettuce-leaf edges makes them heavy and less frilly. A second pass on free-motion satin stitching is extremely difficult but will certainly hone your skill on control and patience.

If you choose to resew an edge, you'll get the best result using a spring hoop holding two pieces of water-soluble stabilizer with the petal sandwiched in between. Complete the stitching, then carefully tear away the stabilizer.

The standard top thread for machine embroidery is usually 30–50 wt., whether it is rayon, cotton, or metallic. This fine thread requires the sewing machine's top tension to be one or two numbers looser than the suggested tension for garment construction. This is a rule of thumb and, with experience, you will learn to judge the tension for each project.

For most appliqué situations, you will wind the bobbin with white cotton thread compatible in weight to the machine-embroidery thread. (See Chapter 1 under Threads Galore.) If you are sewing or embroidering three-dimensional flowers and leaves, use a matching or coordinating color in the bobbin with ten-

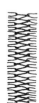

Fig. 2.3 Tension for a good satin stitch shows ⅓ bobbin thread and ⅔ top thread on the wrong side of the fabric.

sion that is normal for that particular thread. If the bobbin thread persists in pulling to the surface of the work, then slightly tighten its tension.

Another method, instead of fusing, is to cut all the appliqué shapes, place them on the background fabric using a dab of glue stick, and cover with a piece of water-soluble stabilizer. After completing the satin stitching, trim the excess stabilizer with scissors and the rest will wash away when you soak or launder the fabric. This process gives a smooth and padded appearance to the satin stitch compared to stitching without stabilizer.

If you want to add a hint of color and texture, cover the project with tulle. The excess can be trimmed easily after completing the stitching. Tulle is available in many colors and, when hooped with the project, will hold the loose appliqué pieces in place.

Decide whether you want to use water-soluble stabilizer or tulle and which machine attachment (or none at all) for free-motion embroidery. You will have better control guiding your work if you use a 5" (127mm) or 7" (178mm) spring hoop in addition to the above choices. With fine wovens, a wooden embroidery hoop is best and will prevent the fabric from puckering. Don't fool yourself into thinking that you can always iron your problems away.

APPLIQUÉ FOOT

An appliqué foot comes with all sewing machines and, like the darning foot, can be metal or plastic. Is is also called an embroidery or an open-toe foot. You can cut away the center section if it is not already an open-toe appliqué foot. Notice the wide opening on the underside, which allows the satin stitching to feed evenly under the foot and out the back (Fig. 2.4). This foot provides pleasing results with decorative machine stitches.

Fig. 2.4 Open-toe appliqué foot (top and bottom view).

DARNING FOOT

A darning foot comes with most sewing machines. The style varies slightly, and generic models are available for all mechines (Fig. 2.5). The metal or clear plastic foot can be customized by cutting away the front section and sanding the opening smooth so that it won't damage fabrics.

The darning foot is to free-motion embroidery what training wheels are to a novice bicycle rider. This foot helps to keep your work from bouncing and assists you in moving the work smoothly while stitching. You will eventually acquire this skill and enjoy stitching without a machine foot.

DARNING SPRING

A darning spring is an attachment that fastens by inserting the needlescrew in the loop. The spring holds the fabric down when the needle stitches into the fabric. I find this is the least stable of all the choices. The darning spring is available at sewing-machine stores and mail-order sources for about $1.00. You might find threading the needle difficult, and the spring tends to give the user a false sense of security because it flexes easily (Fig. 2.6).

SPRING NEEDLE

The spring needle seems to provide the answer to many stitching problems. This needle is designed to attach a spring mechanism to a #80 (12) needle (Fig. 2.7). With care, you can

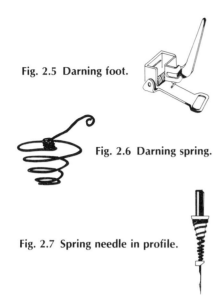

Fig. 2.5 Darning foot.

Fig. 2.6 Darning spring.

Fig. 2.7 Spring needle in profile.

insert a #90 (14) needle, but use that large size only in that particular spring. Spring needles cost about $6.00.

I have found that the older models of Viking sewing machines have a problem with the fabric bouncing even when it is in a hoop. This causes skipped stitches and great frustration if you want to do free-motion embroidery. The Viking also has a darning spring that makes it difficult to see the work in progress. I solve both problems by leaving the shank attached, but I remove the foot and turn the dial, which increases the pressure on the presser foot until the shank is just above the work when the presser bar is down. This procedure can be used for all types of machine embroidery and in place of other attachments.

Other Machine-Stitched Edges

The stretch blind-hem stitch set at a 4 width and a satin-stitch length offers a good alterna-

tive to the standard satin-stitch edging. It provides a strong edge and is more decorative. The scarf edge and overedge stitches are functional but may become a decorative edging when stitched with embroidery threads.

Look through the decorative stitches for your sewing machine and find the ones that will give a satin-stitch finish (Fig. 2.8). You may even find stitches that are usually more open, but, when set for a short length, will cover the appliqué's edge nicely. The stitch used will depend on the size of the appliqué.

Another option instead of satin stitching is to zigzag a cord on the edge of the appliqué. First use a narrow zigzag to stitch around all the cut edges of the appliqué. Then use a foot that allows a single cord to feed in the center, directly in front of the needle (Fig. 2.9). You can make your own by taping a small card with a hole in the center on top of an appliqué foot. You can also feed the cord through a 4″ (102mm) plastic straw and hold it in front of the needle while stitching. This guide for the cord works well when using an appliqué foot, darning foot, or spring needle for free-motion work.

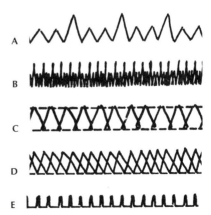

Fig. 2.8 Practical stitches that can be used for decorative edges besides satin stitching: (A) stretch blind hem, (B) stretch blind hem in satin length, (C) double overlock, (D) single overlock, (E) interlock.

Fig. 2.9 Specialty feet with guides for feeding a cord or wire in the center.

You have still another consideration for a decorative edge on appliqués. Combine a double needle with a decorative stitch. The sizes of the double needles go from 1.6 to 4.0 and occasionally are found wider at 6.0 for machines that have a 9mm-wide stitch capacity. My choice for this technique is to use a narrow 2.0 so I won't be too limited on the stitch width. Before you thread the machine, insert the needle and turn the handwheel manually to make sure the needles clear the throat plate for the entire stitch pattern. Using variegated threads or two different colors in the needles will provide a lacelike and creative edge. Use an appliqué foot and keep the feed dogs up.

Gathering Flowers and Leaves

Use the following techniques on your sewing machine or serger to gather the bases of flowers and leaves. These techniques are close to a hand-basting stitch as we can achieve with a machine. (See Figure 10.5 in Chapter 10.)

TECHNIQUES FOR SEWING MACHINES

The important consideration in gathering is that you need a long basting stitch for the best results. The average sewing machine's longest length of about 4mm is not long enough for most cabbage roses.

Bernina sewing machines can be set for a saddle stitch, where the machine will skip every other stitch and produce a very long basting stitch. Elna sewing machines have a basting-plate accessory that will accomplish the same task when using a zigzag stitch.

No matter which method you choose, when you use the machine stitch for a gathering thread, be sure to use a strong construction thread in the needle so it won't break when you pull it. Set a long stitch length and a tight top tension with a normal bobbin tension so that the top thread will pull easily for gathering. The bobbin thread pulls to the top slightly and acts as a casing for the gathering thread.

For light fabrics, you can use a gathering foot, long stitch length, tight top tension, and normal bobbin. This setup will encourage gathering, but you may still want to pull the top thread to increase the gathers.

A great method for gathering starts by taking one stitch into the fabric and pulling the bobbin thread up through the fabric. Depending on the amount of gathering, use a strong thread in the bobbin, such as quilting or #8 pearl cotton. Pull out enough thread so that it is as long as the fabric you will be gathering. Zigzag over this thread, then pull to gather.

Another option is to zigzag over crochet or pearl cotton, thus making a stitched casing for the drawstring. Save yourself some grief and use a foot that will feed the string in the center, in front of the needle. Look through your sewing machine feet and find one with a hole or center guide for cord. New accessory feet made especially for attaching beads, pearls, and sequins will also work for stitching drawstrings and wires in place.

Generic feet with these features are available at sewing-machine stores and through mail order (see Supply Sources). Try using feet from other sewing machines. An adapter may be necessary, but it's worth buying when you see how many unique feet you will have at your service. Otherwise, tape a small section of a drinking straw or plastic coffee stirrer to the top front of the foot to serve as a guide for the gathering cord while sewing it on the fabric.

TECHNIQUES FOR SERGERS

A three-thread serged seam can act as a casing on the edge of the pattern for the Cabbage Rose in Chapter 6 (Fig. 6.2, top). If you have two needles on your serger, use the one in the right needle position and set a 3 length. The differential feed can be set to encourage gathering, but it usually doesn't provide enough fullness for this project, so I keep it on the normal setting. This serged seam will be done over a single strand of crochet or pearl cotton. Some serger feet have a hole in the front through which you thread the cotton. If yours doesn't and you have difficulty guiding the

gathering string while serging, you can weave it in and out of the seam later with a blunt-tipped needle. Pull gathers tight, roll the gathered fabric to form a cabbage rose, and secure with hand-stitching or a glue gun.

Another way to use your serger is to sew a flatlock on the center lengthwise fold on the Cabbage Rose pattern in Chapter 6 (Fig. 6.2, bottom) to make a casing. Follow your machine manual for setting the serger to sew a flatlock. Make sure the serger is sewing a balanced three-thread seam. Turn the needle tension all the way to 0 so the needle thread will have minimal tension (see Figure 10.4).

Fold the fabric strip in half lengthwise with right sides together. Next, serge a flatlock on the fold with a gathering cord inside the fold. Pull the fabric to open flat. Or, weave a gathering cord through the ladder stitch after the serging is done.

3

Fusing, Edges, and Shaping Techniques

This chapter will explain finishing techniques and their variations in detail, as well as the best methods of fusing, edging, or shaping fabric petals. Naturally, you are not limited to a particular method given for each project. The combinations for each of the projects in this book are unlimited. Throughout, I will suggest techniques and supplies that are the most suitable for an initial attempt for each project. Whenever possible, I mention name brands so you can experiment and not have to guess what products give the best results. If any of the supplies trigger an idea or use of another product, I would love to hear about it.

Fusing Methods

Some of the appliquéd flowers in Chapter 4 are fused to the background fabric with fusible web. Fusible web comes in light, medium, and heavy weights and some have a paper backing. Dimensional fabric flowers can be stiffened by fusing the outer and inner layers together for each petal. The degree of stiffness depends on the weight of the fabric, the weight of the fusible web, and the size of the flower. A household iron is adequate for fusing, but a flat press provides a large work surface for layout and for applying even pressure over a larger ironing area. Protect the iron and the ironing or pressing surface from

direct contact with the fusible web by using a Teflon pressing sheet.

LIGHTWEIGHT FUSIBLE WEB

Wonder-Under is a lightweight, paper-backed fusible web. Fine Fuse, also a lightweight web (but not paper-backed), requires the use of a Teflon sheet to protect the iron and ironing board. Since they are lightweight, these two webs will fuse in less than ten seconds.

MEDIUM-WEIGHT FUSIBLE WEB

Stitch Witchery (not paper-backed) has been the popular fusible for many years. Used between Teflon sheets, it will fuse in ten seconds. I place the fabric with the wrong side up and the Stitch Witchery on top of the fabric, then sandwich both between two opaque sheets of Teflon. This method lets you see where the fusing is complete. As with any fusible, if the iron is too hot or held in place for too long, the fabric will scorch. Synthetics and lamés are heat-sensitive and will ripple permanently. (But you might like this snakeskin texture for a different project.)

Heat n Bond Lite, a medium-weight fusible with a paper backing, has a textured surface and fuses in only three to five seconds. This makes the job a snap, but sometimes the texture of the web shows through lightweight fabrics, even when it has been fused properly.

Other brands with paper backing include: Dritz Magic Fuse, HTC Trans-Web, Staple Transfer Fusing, and Aleene's Hot Stitch Fusible Web.

HEAVY-WEIGHT FUSIBLE WEB

A heavier-weight fusible web is the standard Heat n Bond with a paper backing. This product is recommended for craft and nonsewing projects because it is a thin sheet of glue instead of a web layered with paper. When sewing through it, however, the sewing machine needle may become coated with a residue that causes the thread to fray or break. I haven't had this trouble, but always test fabrics before beginning each project. This weight isn't necessary for most appliqués on garments, but it is ideal when you want to increase significantly the stiffness of two fabrics by fusing them together. A large dimensional flower could benefit from the added weight in holding its shape. A purse or tote bag constructed from a double layer of fused fabrics will be sturdy and still easy to sew. This fusible bonds quickly in three to five seconds.

SUCCESSFUL FUSING

During fusing, you need to protect your iron and ironing board from the fusible web. Most notions displays in fabric stores sell packages of a lightweight Teflon pressing sheet, or look for it in assorted thicknesses in stores that sell plastic supplies for sign makers and businesses. My choice is 5-mil, which is a little heavier than a plastic freezer bag. This weight will last longer and is more economical than what you will find in fabric stores. I also use it to cover my work surface when using a glue gun.

Medium-weight fusible web required ten seconds to fuse properly. Use a dry iron on the cotton setting, since the steam cannot

penetrate the Teflon sheet. Rather than ironing back and forth, press in only one area at a time. Pivot the iron in place for even bonding and also to prevent the vent-hole pattern on the iron from transferring to the fabric. Let the fabric cool before peeling away the Teflon sheet. Otherwise, the knit or bias of the fabric will become distorted and ruin the fabric for flat appliqué.

Before using the Teflon sheet again, remove any fusible residue by rubbing your hand over both sides. You don't want to find residue on the bottom of your iron, on the ironing board cover, or transferred to your project or a garment you iron later. Clean the iron with Dritz Iron-off. Melted fusible web can be removed from fabrics and ironing-board covers with denatured alcohol, but the affected areas will show discoloration.

To fuse the appliqué shape to the background fabric, put the shape in place and cover with the Teflon sheet. Press, then replace the Teflon with a light pressing cloth (a bandanna is great) and steam ten seconds for a permanent bond. If you have overlapping shapes or a complicated appliqué with smaller shapes on top, you can do all your fusing on the Teflon sheet to assemble single appliqué. Sandwich between sheets of Teflon. Let cool, then peel it off and do one final fusing to the background fabric.

FUSING MORE THAN FABRIC

Experiment fusing objects that can withstand the heat and are machine washable or can be laundered as the garment requires. These include flat wooden shapes, shisha mirrors, wires, and rhinestones. In addition to fusing other objects to fabric, you can fuse finished appliqué designs to wooden or cardboard surfaces. Leota Black, owner of Ultra Delight in Wheeler, Texas, specializes in Ultrasuede appliqué and offers a few tips when working with rhinestones. Use the prepared, iron-on rhinestones. Hold each rhinestone in place with a piece of Scotch-brand removable tape and cover with a folded wet pressing cloth. Press on a firm, padded surface like a folded terry towel on top of a Formica counter. An ironing board is too cushioned and does not provide an adequate surface for pressing. Press for 30 seconds, let the fabric cool, then press again for 30 seconds. Remove the tape and the rhinestone will remain permanent for many washings. Turn the garment inside out to launder.

Cloth-covered florist wire can be fused successfully to the Suede Minis in Chapter 7 and the English Ivy in Chapter 8. The wire can be precut and shaped to any size before fusing. Cut ⅛" (3.2mm) strips of a light- to medium-weight fusible web. Glue-stick the length of web to the wrong side of the fabric, then fuse as instructed for these two projects.

Edges

Fabric flowers and leaves will hold their shape because of the gathering and assembly involved in securing the fabric pieces together. Adding stitching on the edges will provide not only a decorative touch but also will make a firm trim.

The following edge treatments are presented in the order of convenience and ease of execution. Not all of the edge treatments are appropriate for every kind of fabric or flower, so follow my recommendations accordingly. The emphasis of this book is to use the sewing machine's attachments and stitches. I also include directions for serging an absolutely perfect narrow rolled hem. For creativity's sake, I include edge treatments that can be applied without being stitched. The combination of colors and techniques will give you a rich finish.

CUT EDGES

Cutting an edge of fabric with a regular straight-edged pair of scissors might not seem like the best way to finish woven fabric. But you will have excellent results when cutting edges if they have been painted first or the fabric has been fused. Instead of cutting a plain straight edge, cut a wavy edge, which will cause the petals to undulate. Method B of The Cabbage Rose in Chapter 6 is perfect for this technique (see page 70). This same flower pattern cut on the bias is good for cutting a ¼"-wide (6.3mm) fringe. The fabric will stay intact, unlike a strip cut on the grain, where the fringe would ravel and fall off.

Good old pinking shears or scallop or wavy-edge shears will give any full flower a fluted look, like a carnation. Using these shears on synthetic suedes, tricot, laces, Lycra, and felt offers the perfect combination for a clean-edge finish because the fabrics will not ravel. A wavy or scallop edge decoratively finishes woven fabrics and minimizes raveling. Combine the cut edge with a painted edge for a more dramatic flower. (Painted and dyed petal edges are discussed later in this chapter.)

MANIPULATED EDGES

If you cut the fabric for a cabbage rose on the bias, you can distress the edges by pulling and stretching the fabric. You will find that tugging at the fabric is easier in one direction than the other. Pull on the cut edge as though

Fig. 3.1 Bias strip of fabric with a manipulated edge.

you are trying to make it ravel. The bias cut of the fabric will cause the edge to fray and flute but will not ravel out of control. This ruffled edge is attractive and you need only regular scissors to cut it (Fig. 3.1).

MACHINE-STITCHED EDGES

Chapters 1 and 2 discuss the sewing machine setup and the presser feet that can be used for embroidery and edging. They also cover satin stitching and other built-in stitches that are decorative alternatives for edging. Once you become familiar with these stitches and know how to set up your machine, you will be ready for unlimited creative fun.

LETTUCE LEAF EDGES

When you set your sewing machine for a rolled hem (short length, wide width) and use a hemmer or a rolled edge foot, you can sew a lettuce-leaf edging. A hemmer ensures a consistent stitch while rolling the fabric. You can use an appliqué foot if you feed the fabric slowly, allowing the width of the stitch to roll the fabric since the foot can't do it. This technique works best when sewn on the folded edge of the fabric. Some knits will allow you to stretch and sew a satin stitch on a single cut edge, but be aware that the fabric may run if you pull too hard. Stitching on a bias fold or a bias cut edge of woven fabric gives a mildly fluted edge.

When you cut woven fabric on-grain, you can easily achieve a beautiful rolled edge that will lie flat without ruffling. Use a 4 width, satin-stitch length and an open-toe foot. The full width of the stitch will roll and cover the cut edge evenly with thread as long as the needle swings to the right, just off the edge of the fabric. As mentioned, this same setup will work on the folded edge of knit fabrics and on the bias of wovens, if you stretch the fabric while satin stitching on the edge.

For a more interesting look when stitching a rolled edge on knit or woven edges, use a larger needle, such as #80 (12), thread the machine with two colors of rayon, and set a slightly longer length, since the double threads will fill in faster.

Lettuce-leaf edging caters to very stretchy knits and bias folds on woven fabrics. A synthetic suede is neither of these, but you can still achieve a ruffled edge by stitching on the petal's pattern line using a narrow satin stitch. Cut the petal out close to the stitching. This edge can be stretched and manipulated to produce a soft ruffle. (See Shaping with Fabric Stiffeners later in this chapter for more ideas with faux suede.)

Next, change to a twin needle and double the fun. Select a lacelike decorative stitch and insert a #1.8 or #2.0 twin needle. Try stitching two different patterns close together so the four lines of stitching will appear as a single lace edging on the fabric (Fig. 3.2). Before threading your machine, turn the handwheel manually and watch the needle to make sure it clears the throat plate for the entire stitch pattern. Set your machine for the widest setting possible without causing damage to the needles and machine. Each needle can be threaded with a different color—two shades of one color or one rayon thread and one metallic thread. To prevent tangling, be sure that thread from one spool unwinds from the front of the spool and the other thread unwinds

Fig. 3.2 Stitching sample using a #2.0 twin needle, decorative stitches, and a different color thread in each needle.

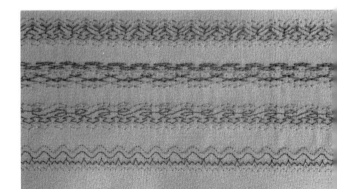

from the back of the spool. Hold the threads together and pass them through all the guides together, with the exception of the tension disc, where the threads will pass on either side. Some machines also have double thread guides on the needle bar.

When you want to edge straight edges or slight curves, use the twin needle to attach narrow ribbons, cording, or yarns instead of using a satin stitch. Look through your assortment of presser feet and see if you have one that will allow for feeding the trim through the center of the foot. (See Chapter 1 for information on presser feet.) If you don't have the appropriate foot to guide the ribbon or cord, use a dab of glue stick to hold the trim in place instead of fussing with straight pins.

SCALLOP EDGES

To make an attractive scalloped edge, thread a double needle with two shades of one color. The thick and thin lines of the stitching will accentuate the gradations of color. The satin stitch flows like calligraphy when you

Fig. 3.3 Scallop edge made with a twin needle, two shades of thread, and free-motion embroidery.

are doing free-motion embroidery to make a scallop edge with a satin stitch (Fig. 3.3).

Machine Setup

Stitch length: 0
Stitch width: 2–4 (depending on the opening in the cover plate)
Feed dogs: down or covered
Presser foot: none or spring needle
Upper tension: looser than normal
Lower tension: normal
Needle size: #2.0 twin needle
Top thread: two shades of the same color, one in each needle
Bobbin thread: one of the colors that is used on top
Hoop: 7" (178mm) or larger spring or wooden

The combination of hooped fabric and a darning foot allows you good control of the work while giving you the freedom to stitch anywhere. First, draw the petal shapes on a piece of fabric with a washout pen. You will cut out the petals after you have done all the stitching. When stitching scallops using free-motion techniques (without a foot or automatic stitch to control the fabric), it is important to exaggerate the original drawn line. Make sure to stitch the point between scallops a little deeper than drawn. If you follow the line exactly, the scallops will appear to go limp and lose their definition.

For edging strips or giant petals, use an appliqué foot and an automatic or programmed scallop stitch. Small petals have tight curves that are difficult to satin stitch with an appliqué foot and an automatic scallop stitch. Stabilize the fabric with one of the methods in Chapter 1 so that the edges finish flat.

WIRED EDGES

If you want to rearrange petals and reshape the leaves surrounding the flowers, the wired-edge technique is for you. Satin-stitch a wire along all the edges of the petals to allow you unlimited shaping. Or, better, use a single wire down the center, which is sufficient for most flower petals and perfect for leaves. This method is not only faster but is easy to do. (See Chapter 8 for instructions for sewing wires on veins and stems.)

Satin stitching around tight curves like those on petals and leaves presents a challenge but offers an opportunity to hone your skills in free-motion machine embroidery. If this challenge appeals to you, then sandwich the cut fabric shape between two layers of water-soluble stabilizer and place it in a spring hoop. The wire is satin stitched on top and shaped as you stitch. It will be easier to make the wire conform to the curves and angles as you approach them. The wire for this method is 24-gauge cloth-covered green or white wire. Because you will be following tight curves, you cannot use an appliqué foot. In fact, your best and only choice is not to use any foot. Hence, the challenge.

Perhaps you aren't in the mood for a challenge but still want a wired-edge finish. Another option will work with most flowers and leaves. Use the fine plastic-coated copper wire that comes in an assortment of colors. Known as "wire-wrapping wire," it is available at electronics stores for under $3.00. Like florist wire, the color doesn't matter because the wire will be completely covered with stitching. It is softer than telephone-cord wire, which can be satin-stitched using an appliqué foot and a 2 to 2½ width. All wires should be cut with wire cutters so the ends remain straight.

The reason for using a fine gauge of wire-wrapping wire is that it will fit into the tiny hole in machine feet. Bernina's embroidery foot has a hole that will allow a cord or wire to feed straight under the needle so you can zigzag over it. Other comparable feet are available by mail order (see Supply Sources).

Set the sewing machine for a 2 to 2-½

width and satin-stitch length. Use a matching color of thread on top and in the bobbin. Bernina's foot allows you to maneuver your way around curves without having to shape the wire by hand. Although adequate for petal and leaf edges, wire-wrapping wire is too limp for flower stems.

MIZUHIKI PAPER-CORD EDGES

An alternative to using wire for veins and edging is a Japanese paper cord known as Mizuhiki (see Supply Sources). It can sometimes be found in Oriental markets and craft stores. These are cords made by twisting and rolling strong paper, starching it for added strength, then covering it with Mylar, plastic, or silk. Niji makes Mizuhiki in 25 colors, including metallic jewel tones and iridescents. These cords are extremely lightweight and flexible but are not rigid enough to hold a bend as wire does. Although the wire can be cut with scissors, wire cutters are recommended.

The petal and leaf shapes are highlighted using Mizuhiki. Hoop a synthetic fabric like nylon organdy. Straight-stitch around the petal and leaf shapes two or three times using rayon for the top and bottom threads (Fig. 3.4). While the fabric is still in the spring hoop, cut out the shapes with a soldering iron. Sandwich the shapes between two pieces of water-soluble stabilizer and place them in a spring hoop. Couch the Mizuhiki over the straight stitching on the edge of each shape with a small zigzag stitch and monofilament thread in the needle. A satin stitch isn't necessary because it would completely cover the decorative cord with stitching. If you happen to sew through the cord, it will not damage the needle. You can even pinch the cord to close up the hole so that it won't be so noticeable.

This is the order of stitching because the rayon thread will not melt, but the monofilament will. Each petal was washed in warm

Fig. 3.4 Tiny nylon organdy flowers with Mizuhiki (Japanese paper cord) zigzagged on the edges of ⅜" (10mm) to ¾" (19mm) petals and leaves. They are glued around LED light buttons for flower centers.

Fig. 3.5 Gingham flower with 25-lb. fish line enclosed in the petal edges.

water, then rolled before being attached to the project with a low-temperature glue gun.

FISH-LINE EDGES

A fish-line edging will create perky flowers like the gingham trio on the straw hat in the color pages. The petals cannot be shaped as those with wire, but the nylon filament will maintain a firm edge through lots of wear and washing. These petals can be individually sewn to a garment. A 25-pound test line or fishing line is suitable for this technique. This weight provides a fine, rounded satin stitch when encased in a fold of fabric. The fishing line cannot be detected since it is lightweight (Fig. 3.5). Fishing line and the nylon cord used in weed trimmers come in heavier weights and can also be used.

Machine Setup

Stitch length: satin-stitch length
Stitch width: 2
Feed dogs: up
Presser foot: appliqué or pintuck
Upper tension: normal
Lower tension: normal
Needle size: #70 (10)
Top thread: rayon
Bobbin thread: matching rayon

Fold a 4" (102mm) circle of sheer fabric over the fishing line and satin stitch, trapping it in the fold. Using matching thread on top and in the bobbin, select a thread that contrasts with the fabric color. Sew as many petals as needed, one after another, but don't cut them apart yet. Run a gathering stitch along the cut edge, continuing from one petal to the next. If you want more than a single layer of petals, start with the bottom layer. Using an appliqué or darning foot, sew across the base of each petal to hold it in place. Overlap the base of those already attached. Use your favorite flower center from Chapter 7 to finish. A fringe foot is used to make the center of the gingham flower in Figure 3.5.

SERGED EDGES

The rolled edge made on a serger can be done using two or three threads. I prefer two. Besides being more economical, using two threads usually gives better results. It has been my experience and disappointment that capable teachers and sewing personalities teach you how to make a rolled edge, but not a perfect one. Since this stitch is meant to be seen on both sides, especially on a lettuce-leaf edge, it is imperative that you make it perfect. Doing it any other way would be like taking a trip to Disneyland and not going on any rides. Or like going to a fabric store without money.

Machine Setup

Stitch length: satin-stitch length
Stitch width: narrow
Presser foot: as manual suggests
(Right) needle thread: normal
Top looper tension: normal to a slightly
  loose
Lower looper tension: very tight
Needle thread: construction thread
Top looper thread: decorative thread
Lower looper thread: construction thread
Needle: compatible for thread and fabric

Serging a narrow rolled edge produces a gorgeous bound edge and is best for straight or only slightly curved edges. The feet and feed dogs on sergers are longer than those on sewing machines and make maneuvering curves an acquired skill. For example, edging a 3″ (76mm) circle is possible, but it isn't fun. Edging a 5″ (127mm) circle is much easier, but it will keep you on your toes. The fabric must be fed in a continuous circular motion (counterclockwise) while serging. So, if you want to serge a rolled edge on individual petals, a larger flower would be appropriate for a costume or a smashing evening dress. You probably couldn't make a quiet entrance wearing flowers of this size.

Before making any changes in threads, tensions, dials, or plates, serge on a piece of fabric for five inches. You want to make sure the stitching is correct before complicating matters with different threads and mechanical changes. Start with a three-thread seam and adjust the tensions until you have an absolutely perfect, flat seam. Refer to your serger manual or to any book on sergers to help you understand tensions for the serger.

If you want to change any or all of the threads, the following procedure is foolproof and painless. That is just what every serger owner loves to hear. Cut the threads to be changed directly above each cone. Replace the cones with new thread and tie the old and new thread by placing the ends together. Tie a single overhand knot, treating the two threads as one. This simple knot will never come out and is superior to the often-suggested square knot. It is a longtime standard in mass-production sewing.

Cut the needle thread just before it goes into the needle's eye. Lift the presser foot. Remember or write down the numbers for the tension settings for the upper and lower loopers. Turn both tensions to zero and slowly pull the looper threads through all the thread guides until the knots are completely through the machine. Return the tension dials to their original settings. Pull the tension disc toward you to release the tension and slowly pull the upper looper thread through the machine until the new thread is in place. Repeat for the lower looper.

Some older machines may not have numbered settings and may have a different tension system. On these machines, threads can be changed easily one at a time.

Before serging, check every thread guide to make sure you have threaded the machine properly. If you pulled the threads slowly through the machine, they usually will stay in place. Rethread the needle and bring all the thread tails under the presser foot and to the left side. This will hold them in place while you take about four stitches to start the chain before inserting the fabric. Serge a few inches on the fabric and make tension adjustments as needed to accommodate the new thread.

If you want to use two threads for the rolled edge, consult your manual to make sure your machine is capable of this setup. For a three-thread rolled edge, the basic principle is that the needle and upper looper tension remain the same as when serging a perfect, flat seam. The lower looper tension is increased to cause the upper looper thread to wrap completely around the edge of the fabric. The fabric will roll to a narrow edge when you change the stitch finger on which the serger chain forms. Your manual will instruct you to move a lever or change a plate and foot. This procedure is different for each machine and a rolled-edge plate and foot may be an accessory, not an item that comes with your serger.

Even though you may be using three threads, you need only use the important color or decorative thread in the top looper, since it wraps around the edge of the fabric. The needle thread and lower looper show very little and you can get away with using similar colors instead of buying three cones of the same color. For an edge with solid coverage, use a yarnlike thread like woolly nylon. Use regular construction thread in the needle and lower looper.

Fine-tune your serger for a perfect rolled edge by tightening the lower looper tension until its thread is visible on the wrong side of your work as a straight stitch. When you have a perfect rolled edge, it should be a challenge to guess which is the top or underside of this serging. When the top looper wraps completely around, the only clue should be on the underside, where the lower looper and needle thread look like two rows of straight stitching lying snugly side by side.

On occasion, some sergers will require that the top looper tension be loosened when you cannot make the lower looper any tighter. The way to trick your machine into a wider range of tensions is to change the lower looper tension to a very low setting of about three and wrap the thread twice around the tension disc. Then increase the tension slowly until the stitch looks good. Clearly, this can be done only on those models where the tension disc is fully accessible.

SIZZLING EDGES

Heat-sealing the edges of synthetic fabrics is one of my favorite ways to trim excess fabric and clean up an edge next to the stitching. A sizzling edge is great on single layers of fine, woven, synthetic fabrics. This technique works well on nylon and polyester fabrics and for cutting trims, such as grosgrain and the wired-edge ribbons. Even light-colored cotton-blend fabrics respond surprisingly well to a sizzled edge. You don't have to bother with trying to control a candle flame that dances with every breath or sigh. We will use a soldering iron with a fine-pointed tip (Fig. 3.6). (See Chapter 1 under Other Tools and Equipment.)

The common fear that you will burn the stitching is unfounded because the fabric has a lower melting point than the rayon thread. Metallic threads also may be used for the stitched edge, but use the soldering iron carefully if you have added a synthetic thread for iridescence.

Using a soldering iron has many advantages

Fig. 3.6 Soldering irons with assorted tips and holder.

and by no means is intended to be the lazy solution. A heat-sealed edge is strong, will not ravel, and is machine-washable and usually invisible. In addition, it is fast to complete. This is a great combination if you keep tabs on the actual sizzling. As when using a hot glue gun, a healthy fear of getting burned keeps me safety-conscious. Always follow all manufacturer's safety instructions when using a soldering iron.

Successful edges depend on using a clean soldering iron. New irons are tinned before using with solder to prevent oxidation. The tinning might leave residue on the fabric, so always test it on a sample first. On the other hand, if you buy a soldering iron for use only on fabrics, it will not have been tinned and thus will not be good for other kinds of soldering. Some soldering irons come with a sponge and instructions for using it to clean residue from the iron. Do so often. Blackened residue will build up on the tip of the soldering iron from melted fibers and may ruin the edge of fabric you are trimming. Unplug the iron and, while it is still hot, carefully rub a wad of aluminum foil on the tip to remove the goop. Next, clean the tip with a small amount of Dritz Iron-off and a paper towel folded several times.

Use the finest needle-point or pencil-point tip for cutting out shapes. A larger tip is clumsy and makes a mess, melting lots of fabric as you try to maneuver. A flat-blade tip is useful if you want to cut larger shapes without sewing the edges first. Place the fabric on top of a Teflon or glass surface. Use the soldering iron as soon as it is hot. If it heats for long periods of time, you will have trouble moving the iron fast enough to prevent blackened edges from excessive melting. Most of the time, you won't have to worry about the odors from melted synthetic ribbons or fabrics. If you anticipate extended use of a soldering iron, set an electric fan in your work area to blow away the odors.

Here is another variation on Murphy's Law: A hot soldering iron will always roll in the direction to inflict the most pain or damage. Get a stand for the soldering iron to prevent accidents. A stand is useful while the iron is heating up as well as cooling so you can work in the area with less worry. Even when you are careful, a kink in the cord may cause the soldering iron to roll in the wrong direction if it is bumped accidently.

A piece of glass or mirror makes an ideal cutting surface when using a soldering iron. Residue can be removed easily from the glass with window cleaner or scraped with a sharp blade. For small projects, use the magnified side of a hand mirror. (Although the residue can be easily removed, the mirror is likely to be scratched.) Clotilde makes a cutting surface that is a thin nonstick sheet made of fiberglass impregnated with Teflon; the sheet can withstand temperatures up to 500 degress Fahrenheit. The 18" × 21" (.46m × .53m) size provides a large enough work area for using a soldering iron and hot glue gun. You can cut directly on the sheet without damage. If you hold the soldering iron in one place for longer than ten seconds, the heat may damage the table underneath. In a pinch, use a clipboard with a Masonite surface. This is sufficient for cutting ribbons or when you need only a small work area and don't mind the scent of burned wood.

When cutting out individual shapes, complete the stitching first. Stitch two to three rows of straight stitching on the outline of the shape to be cut out. This will give a simple clean edge, compared to the heavy look of a satin stitch. A sizzled edge is the best solution for all sizes of shapes and is particularly good for tiny or detailed pieces. Put the fabric in a spring hoop to hold the fabric taut while using the soldering iron. Rest it on the table to hold it steady. Once the iron is hot, you need to apply only slight pressure to cut the fabric. Pushing too hard or trying to melt away large

Fig. 3.7 Ultrasuede roses by Dale Roybal of San Diego, California, using techniques by Shirley Smith for edging with a candle flame and paraffin shaping.

areas of fabric will leave a buildup of black, melted fabric on the tip. It will either fall onto the fabric and ruin the work or fall on your skin and burn for what seems like forever. Try to cut inside any drawn lines, since the pencil or ink may darken when it contacts the heat.

Shapes up to $\frac{1}{4}$" (6.4mm) across can be melted away. For larger shapes, cut along one side with the soldering iron, then grip this flap with your fingers or a pair of bent-nose tweezers. Hold the flap with a gentle tension while you continue to cut out the rest of the shape.

I have experimented with using a soldering iron to cut and texture edges of Ultrasuede, but this fabric melts too fast and makes cutting smooth edges difficult, especially for small shapes. It is interesting that light colors melt to glasslike jewel colors when seared. Dark colors like cranberry and purple will turn black. Shirley Smith of Denver, Colorado, uses a candle flame 1" (25mm) from the petals to sear the edges (Fig. 3.7). The darkened edge gradually feathers to the natural color of the fabric. Stretch the edge to a slight ruffle while it is hot. Wear cotton garden gloves if the fabric is too hot to handle.

CHEMICALLY SEALED EDGES

Sealing an edge chemically may sound intimidating and something you may prefer not to fool with. Actually, it is the best description for items you may already have among your sewing or craft supplies. The first item is a seam sealant such as Fray Check, Fray No More, or Aleene's Stop Fraying. These are used primarily to seal the stitching at the beginning or ends of seams and are machine-washable. They will be referred to as "seam sealants" throughout the book. Edge a sample with a sealant and see if this method will be compatible with your fabric before investing precious time and materials. These products have a tendency to discolor some fabrics and threads. Use a paint brush to apply a sealant to the edges. To clean, wash the brush with warm water and soap while it is still wet. To make a fine line, use a Tip-Pen on the end of the seam sealant container. See Fabric Paints, Dyes, and Inks, below, for further information on these metal tips.

Fabric prints of jungle animals, fish, and florals have a painterly blending or colors and these cutouts make colorful appliqués. Unfortunately, a satin-stich edge is too bold and makes them look like patches. For a more artistic finish, fuse the cutouts to the background, paint a seam sealant on the cut edges, for extra insurance, then zigzag on the edge with a 1 length and 1 width. This tiny stitch ensures that the appliqué will lie flat, and it won't detract from the print. For example, the floral design of a printed fabric is more important than the edging used to secure it to the background.

An alternative adhesive is Unique Stitch, which comes in a tube. It dries translucent and has a soft, rubberlike touch when dry. This may matter on garments, where other seam sealants sometimes feel scratchy.

Among the usable supplies you may have at home are clear fingernail polish and assorted clear finishes used to gloss or satin-finish projects. These may be thinned and applied to fabric with a paint brush. Craft stores that specialize in fabric painting may sell empty squeeze bottles with needle-point tips for use instead of a paint brush.

Fabric Paints, Dyes, and Inks

I once had reservations about including this method of edging petals and leaves with paints or dyes. The use of fabric paints and glitters is so crafty and so widely promoted that appliqués finished with paint instead of stitching look alike. I generally dislike trendy ideas because these projects sometimes lose their character and uniqueness. But I was pleasantly surprised when I experimented.

The coloration techniques described next are applied to the cut edges before any stitching is added to the petals or leaves. It may be easier to draw all the shapes on the fabric, apply the color, hoop the fabric, add stitching—then cut or burn out the shapes.

FABRIC PAINTS

I experimented with fabric paints and glitters to create a classic bouquet. Because of the popularity of painted garments, numerous brands and a multitude of paint colors are easily found in craft and fabric stores. There is even a neon-colored glue that can be used like fabric paints. The quality of slick and glitter paints has greatly improved. Special needle-point tips can be added to squeeze bottles to produce a fine painted line. Tip-Pens by Advantage Products are metal tips in four sizes that screw directly on the bottle or on the extension caps that serve as adapters. Besides using them with fabric paints, they facilitate working with seam sealants, fabric and craft glues, candy icing and even with fingernail decorating (see Supply Sources).

With practice, you will achieve a steady hand for squeezing paints on petal or leaf edges. Make a beaded edge more interesting by squeezing on dots of paint instead of a smooth line. Either edge may dry with a raised finish or may be pressed flat with an iron when it is tacky.

Protect your iron and ironing board with foil and use a medium heat setting on the iron. Whether you paint one or both sides of the petal, you may cut the petal after pressing the paint flat. Use pinking or scalloping shears to recut a painted edge. If you have the patience, cut a painted fringe edge with regular scissors or use a button-hole chisel to make carnations, bachelor buttons, or cornflowers.

Another painted edge can be done using artist's acrylic paint and a brush. Like the fabric paints, acrylics can be thinned and cleaned up with water. They also dry permanently and do not require curing or heat-setting.

You probably expect paint to be a liquid or fluid substance; however, you will have exciting results when you try Paintstik Markers by Delta/Shiva. These paints were used on the Suede Minis in Chapter 7 and could also be used on the felt Cactus Dish Garden in Chapter 6. They are nontoxic and hypo-allergenic oil-based sticks whose color can be applied by coloring directly on the fabric or by using a stencil brush. The 85 colors include artists' colors, glitters, and iridescents. They blend smoothly and seldom turn muddy from overblending. On napped fabrics, use a Japanese Bunka brush for further blending. Paintstiks clean up with soap and water and dry in 48 to 72 hours. The colors seem permanent but can be heat-set with an iron for machine washing as directed by the manufacturer.

Color directly on the fabric or place a stencil on top and draw on the outline of the stencil's edge. Using a stencil brush with a flat top, brush a circular motion, pulling the color from the stencil onto the fabric. To achieve a watercolor effect, dip a brush in turpentine to make a wash. You will like using the new odorless turpentine.

DYES AND INKS

Dyes and inks, unlike fabric paints, are usually thought of as artist supplies rather than craft supplies. I would never say that one is better than the other, but the popularity of craft supplies makes fabric paints readily available. The dyes and inks I will discuss have specific uses and may not be available in craft or fabric stores.

Dyes and inks may be applied with a paint brush or cosmetic wedge sponge, or they may come ready to use in a pen. These felt, fiber, or ball-tipped pens are an easy way to color the inner petal centers or to shade the petal edges. Veins on the leaves can also be added in ink and accented with stitching.

Felt pens are either nonpermanent or permanent when used on fabric. Features include brush tips, broad points, fine points, and of course an array of colors. Fabric and craft stores carry a basic color assortment of permanent fabric pens used primarily for coloring fabric. Manufacturers recommend that the fabric be prewashed and have a minimum cotton content of 25 percent.

Quilt shops and office supply stores usually carry Pigma Micron pens, which are fiber-tipped. Like technical pens, the black pens come in an assortment of nib sizes. They are permanent pens and their basic crayon-box colors are available in the finer points. This Japanese pen is the finest, most permanent pen available. It is used for dedicating and signing quilts instead of embroidering the wording. They are also the favorite pens for making doll faces.

Architects and commercial artists use a variety of fiber and ball-tipped pens. Artist supply stores carry both nonpermanent and permanent ink pens. Your choice of pen depends on how you will display your fabric flowers and whether you will want to launder them. Nonpermanent pens have many purposes and come in all price ranges. You can find inexpensive assortment packs for a few dollars, as well as washable brilliant and pastel pens for children to use. These pens can be used on fabrics and the hard lines can be blended with a damp paint brush. Broad-tipped pens are more efficient to use than those that resemble a pencil point. Petals colored with permanent pens can be blended with a brush dipped in alcohol or nail-polish remover. Test a fabric sample first because synthetics may react negatively to the solvents and the fabric may crinkle. Be sure to work with your "mistakes"—you could have created something wonderful!

Before adding color to the petals and leaves, look at real plants. You will learn the most from nature and will make better color choices. Edging colors may include shades of rust, wine, forest green, or charcoal. Inner petals might be colored with lime, yellow, lavender, fuchsia, or even a black walnut brown after you have added a brilliant dimensional center. Doesn't the latter combination sound like a poppy?

Other dyes include those used for tie-dying and silk painting. These dyes may have limited applications, since the best results depend on fabric content. One drawback is that you might stifle your spontaneity if you don't have any 100 percent silk or cotton among your fabric stash. These two natural fabrics are used predominantly with dyes because they absorb and retain the most color. Experiment, too, with other natural fibers and blends. Dipping petals in diluted solutions will produce subtle results. Even compromised results can be rewarding. I suggest these dyes because you might have some on hand from a textile class. Now they await your rediscovery.

Shaping with Fabric Stiffeners

After having made a few flowers and leaves, you will realize that the same flower pattern may be used for different kinds of flowers by simply shaping the petals to curl in various directions.

The following methods for shaping petals and leaves are suggested for flowers that will not be stitched to garments. These flowers should be dusted or blown instead of washed. The shaping is preserved but is not apparent until you touch the stiffened fabric. The results are classic but are not for every flower, since the technique must be appropriate for the fabrics used. These stiffeners would also be appropriate for the Stiffened Fabric Sack vases in Chapter 10.

Use a layer of foil to protect your work area from any of the stiffeners. Foil can also be used to hold the fabric shapes in place when molded. Once you moisten the individual shapes with the appropriate stiffener, you can stretch, roll, bundle, or pleat them before they are completely dry. Water-based stiffeners usually air-dry, but you can also use a hair dryer or heated oven that has been turned off. Tools for shaping include a curling iron, a hair crimper, and a puff iron with its oval ironing surface. The shapes should be almost dry so the stiffener doesn't make a mess.

Your choice of stiffener will determine whether you stiffen the flower before or after assembling the petals.

PARAFFIN

An unusual method of shaping fabric flowers is the process of applying ordinary grocery-store paraffin to the wrong side of the fabric. The fabric must be able to withstand the heat of an iron on a cotton setting and should be thick enough so the paraffin does not penetrate it. The fabric best suited to this technique is Ultrasuede. This technique was developed by Shirley Smith of Denver, Colorado, who also sears the edges of flowers with a candle flame (see Fig. 3.7).

This method of stiffening and shaping petals before assembly works best with Ultrasuede and Facile. Protect the ironing board with a paper towel or a brown paper bag. Steam the petal on the wrong side, holding the iron above the fabric without touching it. Then rub it with paraffin. The fabric will absorb the wax and you can steam the petal again with a light pressure on the iron. Apply the wax three or four more times, depending on the desired stiffness. While the petal is warm, stretch and shape the petal with the right side facing you. This type of flower is best assembled by wiring together at its center. (See Chapter 7 for flower centers and Chapter 8 for more finishing ideas.)

STARCHING METHODS

Once you have assembled a fabric flower, you can still stiffen it if you feel that this will enhance its presentation. Usually it is easier to apply the stiffener to the components before assembling them into a flower. If starching is an afterthought, you can still do it carefully to a completed flower using the traditional liquid starch or sugar-water solution. The following starch solutions can be diluted, so you can dip the flower, or they can be thinned even more, so you can apply the solution with a spray bottle or paint brush.

Make a few sample petals and try them with your choice of stiffener. Some fabrics will give better results with different starches. Generally, satin-finish and napped fabrics won't like any of them. Remember that if you have painted or dyed the fabric with water-based inks, use hair spray or paraffin or test commercial sprays as the shaping medium.

After using any of the stiffeners, let the fabric shapes air-dry until damp. Shape the petals or leaves and pin to Styrofoam or foil if necessary. Both of these materials can be cut and shaped to make reusable molds for drying. Continue to air-dry the shapes or use a hair dryer.

CRAFT FABRIC STIFFENERS

Most fabric stiffeners like Aleene's and Mod Podge can be diluted with water or with any thin white craft glue to the proper consistency for spraying or painting. If you want a hard finish and want to saturate fabric with a thicker solution, pour the undiluted stiffener into a heavy resealable bag. Put flowers or petals into the bag and massage the fabric thoroughly. Squeeze the excess stiffener from the fabric as you remove it from the plastic bag. Snip a corner on the bag and squeeze the leftover liquid into the original container.

For a high-gloss finish, use clear acrylic paint medium as a stiffener. You may need to apply two coats, depending on the fabric. Use the medium in a resealable plastic bag, as instructed above, or paint it on the fabric.

SUGAR-STARCH RECIPE

This sugar-starch recipe originated with Carol Duvall, a craft expert on a morning television show. She suggested it as a paste for stiffening fabric strips to be made into bows for packages and decorations. I like the feel and inconspicuous stiffness this recipe provides.

In a Teflon-coated saucepan, mix 1 cup cold water with 4 tablespoons flour. Mix thoroughly as you would for making gravy—no lumps! Slowly add 1 cup hot water and bring to a boil. Remove from the heat and add 1-½ tablespoons sugar. Place the fabric pieces on a piece of foil for easy cleanup. Coat the fabric with the hot paste using a wide brush.

Make sure that the paste soaks through the fabric. The fabric dries evenly in about thirty minutes on a warm day when the pieces are hung to dry. Sewn shapes like the circle leaves in Chapter 8 keep their bubble shape when saturated and hung for air-drying.

WATER-SOLUBLE STABILIZER

If you use water-soluble stabilizer for machine embroidery, save the scraps! Dissolve them in hot water and use this starching solution for dipping or spraying fabric flowers. Allow them to air-dry or use a hair dryer. Or mist the flowers with a spray bottle filled with this solution, allow them to dry, and repeat as many times as needed. Make sure to test your fabric.

When you make the Lacelike Flowers in Chapter 5 or the Machine-Stitched Leaf Spray in Chapter 8, you will use water-soluble stabilizer to shape the embroidered pieces. Layers of this thin film are trapped within the embroidery and will wash out until they are no longer visible. Upon drying, you will realize that it takes a thorough soaking in lots of clean water to remove the water-soluble stabilizer completely. Of all the shaping methods, this may be the easiest one to work with, since it is both liquid and odorless. Pat the excess moisture with terry towels. The stabilizer solution will wash out completely. Dry the shapes and pin them to a mold as described earlier in this chapter.

LAUNDRY STARCH

Grocery stores carry starch in aerosol cans and spray bottles, as well as a concentrate in quart bottles. If you are serious about starching, consider only the blue concentrate. This starch tends to leave a marbling pattern on dark colors, but it is a great starch. Spray starch works well if you starch the fabric shapes several times, allowing them to dry completely between applications. This is time-consuming, but you can speed it up by using a hair dryer. The aerosol also works well, but the fine mist will settle all over your work area. To prevent flaking, mist the fabric with water first, then use the spray starch.

HAIR SPRAY AND OTHER SEALANTS

Hair spray is a convenient way to stiffen fabric shapes, but it should be applied several times, with thorough drying between applications. If the scent is irritating, try unscented hair spray, which comes in both aerosol cans and spray bottles. Hair spray will stiffen the fabric shapes as well as add a thin lacquer finish, and it's a good sealer for flowers with water-based inks.

If you prefer the convenience of spraying and have a well-ventilated area, several clear sealants available at hardware stores can be applied to fabric.

Dried Floral Spray by TAC is designed to waterproof, preserve, and strengthen dried foliage. The manufacturer claims its clear, matte finish reduces sun fading. It is nontoxic and available from Clotilde's mail order. I like the fabric's finish when treated with this spray in a pump bottle.

Fabric Stiffener by Flor Ever is a waterproof aerosol used by florists to transform limp fabrics and ribbons by adding sizing. This stiffener must be used in a well-ventilated area.

4

Appliquéd Flowers and Leaves

The technique of appliqué has a long history and can be as simple as cutting out bold shapes of fabric and satin stitching them to a background fabric. The current trend is to use floral, jungle, or holiday fabric prints for these appliqué shapes. All these fabrics are attractive, but I want to approach appliqué from a different angle.

Appliqué is the technique of applying fabric to fabric. The projects in this chapter offer creative ways with appliqué that involve a variety of fabrics and do not necessarily use a satin stitch. They include working with silk flowers, faux suede, trapunto or padded appliqué techniques, and making ribbon flowers (Fig. 4.1).

Fig. 4.1 Cardigan jacket made by splitting a sweatshirt, by Sylvia Polk of Fairfield, California, with embellishing techniques created by Philip Pepper and Bambi Stalder.

Fig. 4.2 Silhouettes of silk flowers and leaves help you appreciate the different shapes.

Silk Flowers

The term "silk flowers" is not at all accurate for these lifelike fabric flowers, since they are made of synthetic fabric and not silk. However, calling them "artificial flowers" doesn't do them justice and may give the impression of the awful plastic flowers that preceded them.

The many varieties of silk flowers readily available at craft stores offer many possibilities. When selecting flowers, consider using different sizes, since you can layer three or four to complete one flower. I sometimes take apart old silk flower arrangements and use the flowers for embroidery projects (Fig. 4.2).

PROJECT: SHADOW APPLIQUÉ

Shadow embroidery with silk flowers is a perfect technique for garments with a yoke or a border, or for a border on towels (Fig. 4.3). Like traditional shadow appliqué, where a colored fabric is placed beneath a sheer, the silk flowers will be on top of the background fabric with a layer of sheer fabric over the entire yoke or border area. The flowers will be flat when they are appliquéd.

1 Strip all plastic and wire from the silk flowers and leaves. You will find that carnations, daisies, and chrysanthemums have numerous layers and will make several appliqués. To start with clean flowers, place all the pieces in a lingerie bag and include it with your next load of laundry to be washed and dried. The flowers are colorfast and will not ravel.

2 Place the laundered flowers face down on an ironing board. Cover with a press cloth and steam press to flatten them.

3 Lay the flowers in the yoke or border area. To make hooping easier, you may want to draw the yoke outline on the fabric and cut it out after completing embroidery. Arrange the largest flowers on the garment or background fabric. Keep them not farther than ¼" (6.4mm) to ½" (13mm) apart or they will appear as patches instead of a pleasing composition. You can also overlap the flowers.

4 Layer two or three smaller flowers on top of each large one (Fig. 4.4). If you have planned a special flower center from Chapter 7, then a single flower may be sufficient.

5 Insert leaves under the large flowers. If necessary, cut the base of the leaf so you can tuck it farther under the flower. Sometimes you will need only a touch of greenery, especially if the leaf color is too harsh for your project. Many times the awkward placement of leaves will ruin an otherwise successful arrangement. You will make a safe choice if you position the leaves to point to the flower center. (See Chapter 8 for further information on leaves.)

In the background you can include tiny ¼" (6.4mm) silk flowers such as Baby's Breath or Lily of the Valley. Small cutout dots or shapes

Fig. 4.3 Shadow appliqué band on a washcloth, with detail.

Fig. 4.4 Different silk flowers can be combined to make a single flower.

from lamé can be used to create a background pattern.

6 Generously cover the entire area with a sheer white or off-white fabric. Nylon organdy, sparkle organza, or crystalline are popular choices. Some sheers aren't quite transparent enough to allow the flower colors and shapes to show through, while others are so transparent that you won't get a delicate shadow effect. You will have to experiment to find the fabric you want.

Machine Setup

Stitch length: 0
Stitch width: 0
Feed dogs: down or covered
Preser foot: none, darning foot, or spring needle
Upper tension: looser than normal
Lower tension: normal or slightly tighter
Needle size: #70 (10)-#80 (12)
Top thread: rayon
Bobbin thread: regular
Hoop: 5"–7" (127mm–178mm) spring

Supplies

assortment of silk flowers, sheer fabric, ⅛" ribbon, glue stick, and background-fabric

7 Use a spring hoop and a meandering stitch to machine embroider the background, trying not to overlap stitches. This work is free-motion embroidery, so the squiggle stitches may vary according to your mood. This type of embroidery is similar to the echo stitch used by quilters. The rows are parallel

and echo the outlined shapes of the flowers. Have fun with the freedom and include your name or a special message in the background (Fig. 4.5).

Fig. 4.5 Echo stitching on shadow appliqué with a sewing machine.

Choose an embroidery thread color that will enhance the flowers and not distract from them. Outline the flowers with this same thread. Use the same color for some of the flower centers to give your composition consistency. Bartack flowers on the Cactus Dish Garden in Chapter 6 are good centers for shadow-embroidery centers.

8 When you finish the embroidery, cut out the yoke for the garment. If you are making a border, use a narrow zigzag and stitch on the border lines. For towels, wrap the sheer fabric to the backside and turn the edges under for a clean, narrow finish. Trim the excess sheer fabric on the top side, next to the stitching. Finish these top and bottom edges by covering the zigzag with ⅛" (3.2mm) satin ribbon. Glue-stick in place; then topstitch. A #2.0 double needle works great.

THREE-DIMENSIONAL TECHNIQUES

Because silk flowers don't ravel, you can secure them with minimal stitching radiating from the base of the petals. The thread color you choose can highlight the colors printed

Fig. 4.6 Silk flowers stitched onto a boatneck T-shirt using only a straight stitch.

on the flower (Fig. 4.6). Arch the petals and stitch the tips down for a simple lift. Full flowers such as daisies, carnations, and chrysanthemums are composed of several layers of petals. You can cut a layer of petals open and add tucks or gather two or three layers of petals to make a full flower. A single flower can be pinched at the center and stitched down with green thread to form the calyx for a bloom that hasn't fully opened. A pinch of stuffing under a leaf or petal will add dimension, but you need to stitch around to hold it in place.

Your silk flower garden will be in full bloom before you know it (Fig. 4.7). The garden washes without a fuss and provides a fresh floral touch to pillows, hat bands, or garments.

Fig. 4.7 Assorted three-dimensional techniques for applying silk flowers. Some can also be used with Ultrasuede.

Faux Suede

Imitation suede and chamois fabrics come in different qualities with a price range of $5 to $50 a yard. Like me, you will probably want to try to make the cheaper fabric work before investing in a more expensive fabric. However, once you have the chance to work with Ultrasuede, you will truly appreciate the quality and ease of use despite the price.

Ultrasuede, Caress, Facile, and Ultraleather are among the more expensive synthetics in fabric stores. You haven't lived until you have worked with these fabrics. Actually, it's not work; it's play! Keep in mind that one yard of these fabrics weighs approximately one pound and costs about $50. Most sources that sell these brand-name scraps do so by the pound. The price varies from $20 to $30 a pound, with the higher price for larger scraps or better color assortment (see Supply Sources).

The best sale price for Ultrasuede in fabric stores is in the mid-$30 range. When the fabric is on sale, you might get together with a few friends and each buy several colors and then share the fabric. This way you will have large pieces to work with while paying only "scrap" prices. Now you have become an educated faux-suede scrap hunter.

The following techniques cater to the wonderful qualities of this pricy suede cloth. You can experiment with other fabrics with similar characteristics, such as felt, 100 percent polyester double knit, assorted weights of nylon Lycra, and some vinyls. The fabric should be nonraveling, may have a suggested grain but can be cut in any direction, and will not run when stretched.

Leather punches, a buttonhole knife, and an X-acto knife are good tools for accurately cutting uniform holes or patterns. Leather tool suppliers will suggest a Poundo pad, which allows the punch to penetrate slightly to ensure a clean cut. Use a rawhide mallet on the punches and place the pad on a firm surface such as a cement or granite slab. For detailed cutting, you will find a quality 5" (127mm) scissors easier to maneuver than shears.

PROJECT: FLAT APPLIQUÉ

Select a flower pattern for your appliqué. Prepare the garment, picture, or home-decorator item by stitching a texture on the background fabric. Use your sewing machine's automatic stitches and a thread that will complement or contrast with the fabric. The design may swirl behind the flowers or reflect the petal shapes by following their outline.

When using synthetic suede fabrics for appliqués, you can't trace patterns because the fabric is not transparent. If you intend to fuse the shapes in place, use a paper-backed fusible web. Trace the appliqué shape backward on the paper side; then fuse the web to the wrong side of the fabric with a dry iron. Cut out the appliqué and fuse it to the background fabric using steam and a wet press cloth.

You can cut multiple pieces of the same pattern in three ways: (1) tracing around a template, then cutting; (2) cutting around a template that is attached to the fabric; or (3) cutting on the drawn iron-on transfer line.

If you need to cut several appliqués of the same shape or want to use a fusible without paper backing, cut a template from light cardboard or a similar weight plastic. Templates come in handy for future appliqué projects. After fusing the web to the fabric, trace around the templates on the wrong side of the fabric using a washout pen or a superfine Pigma Micron pen. Cut the shapes inside the drawn line, in case the ink might show later.

Leota Black, the designer of more than 30 appliqué patterns for Ultrasuede, suggests drawing the appliqué shape on freezer paper and pressing it to the wrong side of the fabric. Cut out the shape on the drawn line. The freezer paper pattern is reusable.

The third method is to use a Sulky heat-transfer pen. Trace the appliqué pattern on any plain paper. Use the polyester setting on a dry iron to press the transfer on the wrong side of the fabric. If you want a dark transfer line, press for five seconds with a hotter iron for best results. The permanent line will not show on flat appliqués because of the thickness of Ultrasuede. For dimensional appliqués, you will want to trim away the transfer lines or make sure they are covered with stitching. (See Chapter 1 for other details about transfer methods.)

When using an Ultrasuede fabric for basic, flat appliqué, most of the time you will use an appliqué foot. For free-motion work, you will use a darning foot or spring needle. Choose rayon or cotton embroidery thread to match the appliqué color, and use a small zigzag stitch and a #70 (10) needle. If you have problems with skipped stitches, a #75 (11) stretch needle will solve that problem. The blue coating on the needle is used only for identification. Performance is not affected when the coating wears away. Although a satin stitch is often used for dimensional appliqués, it is not necessary for flat appliqués because the synthetic suede doesn't ravel and any dense stitching could weaken the fabric. If you decide to attach petals or leaves by stitching down only the center veins, use a tapered satin stitch with a graceful curve. Detailed cuts or thin strips of faux suede may be secured with a straight stitch when a zigzag is too clumsy to maneuver. Glue-stick the strips to the background and use a darning foot or spring needle with the fabric hooped.

Machine Setup

Stitch length: 1-½ to 2
Stitch width: 1-½ to 2
Feed dogs: up

Presser foot: appliqué
Upper tension: slightly looser than normal
Lower tension: normal
Needle size: #70 (10) or #75 (11) stretch
Top thread: machine embroidery
Bobbin: regular
Hoop: none
Stabilizer: see Chapter 2 for working on woven and knit fabrics

Supplies

As with other fabrics, I like the ease of appliquéing pieces that have been fused in place (Fig. 4.8). (Chapter 3 explains fusing materials and techniques.) Leota Black, owner of Ultra

Fig. 4.8 Ultrasuede appliqué by Leota Black of Wheeler, Texas, with machine beading and three-dimensional petals.

Delight, suggests that flat appliqués be assembled and temporarily fused to a Teflon sheet. Peel off the assembly as a unit after it has cooled; then fuse it to the background using steam and a wet press cloth. Rhinestones can be fused to Ultrasuede after the embroidery is finished. (See Supply Source for materials and patterns.)

THREE-DIMENSIONAL TECHNIQUES

Many of the dimensional techniques used with silk flowers can be applied to flowers made from faux or imitation suede. The size of the flower and the thickness of the fabric will determine which ones will work. Top-quality suede fabric gives a beautiful cut edge that doesn't require stitching to prevent raveling. A satin-stitched edge will detract from this luxurious fabric. Chapter 3 explains how to execute an assortment of edges and ways to shape and stiffen petals using this particular fabric. Ultrasuede is superior for cutting narrow fringe, as well as for cutting details without having to worry about weakening the fabric.

Three-dimensional Ultrasuede flowers sewn to the background should be simple flowers with only a few petals, such as a hibiscus, fuchsia, pansy, or poppy. Not all the petals have to be 3-D. Those in the background can be sewn like a flat appliqué, with only a few dimensional petals in the foreground. The dimensional petals are edged on top of a hooped piece of water-soluble stabilizer and may be attached to the project with straight stitching.

The satin stitching can be done on hooped Ultrasuede fabric before cutting out the petals. If you want to buy the minimum amount of fabric because of it's high price, you will need only 5" (127mm) to fit into a 5" (127mm) spring hoop. Nyla James of Spring Valley, California, suggests this method of stitching, then cutting, for fluting the edges. Stretch the edges

after satin stitching them (Fig. 4.9, left). If you want to satin stitch precut petals, sandwich them between two layers of water-soluble stabilizer and place in a spring hoop. These petals will not stretch, but you will be able to cover the edge completely with stitching (Fig. 4.9, right).

Fig. 4.9 (Left) Fluted edges on Ultrasuede. (Right) Flat edges on Ultrasuede. Both are satin stitched.

The pansy lapel pin in Figure 4.10 was made using an appliqué pattern from *Elegant Way to Appliqué* (Vol. 1) by Libby Tower. The shapes were cut out, then placed between two hooped pieces of water-soluble stabilizer and edged with a satin stitch. Each petal was sewn to a scrap of Ultrasuede serving as the background. Leaves were added last; then the background was cut away close to the stitching. A tie tack was glued to the back using craft glue.

For larger flowers, fold each petal length-

Fig. 4.10 Dimensional pansy lapel pin made from Ultrasuede using an appliqué pattern.

wise with right sides together and straight-stitch pintucks on each fold. The tucks enable the petals to stand upright.

The Suede Minis in Chapter 7 make dainty centers for Ultrasuede appliqué flowers. As florets, they are in their own miniature world and make an intriguing bouquet. Suede Minis are dimensional and require minimal sewing. The construction time is primarily in the cutting. Use enlarged Suede Mini patterns for the appliqué.

Trapunto and More

Trapunto is the Italian word for "padded." Traditionally, trapunto was hand-appliqué work that was padded by making a slash in the back of each appliqué and inserting stuffing. Then the slit was closed with a whip stitch. With a little planning, you can pad each section while the appliqué is in progress. The following technique is a fun and flowery approach to making a padded appliqué.

Flat appliqué can be enhanced with a thin layer of batting or fleece. You will find different kinds of padding in fabric stores. Press a fusible web on the wrong side of the appliqué fabric and cut out the desired shape. Cut the stuffing 1/4" (6.4mm) smaller on all sides than the appliqué shape. Press or pin each appliqué in place, starting with the one that appears farthest away. Complete the satin stitching in the same order.

In addition to trapunto, this chapter on appliqué will include flowers whose petals are formed by folding a piece of fabric and flowers made with ribbon loops.

PROJECT: PUFFED PETAL FLOWER

The Puffed Petal Flower is a combination of a flat background flower and five stuffed petals appliquéd on top (Fig. 4.11). Ten petals are offset so they are all visible. These flowers are a graceful complement to sweaters.

First, refer to Chapter 3 for sewing on knits to help you prepare the background garment or fabric for the appliqué. I used a washable basting tape found in fabric stores. The tape is either 1/8" (3.2mm) or 1/4" (6.4mm) wide and will not gum up the needle. The 1/8" (3.2mm) wide is best for this project. Whether you use a satin-finish fabric or a cotton print, the garment will take on a new personality.

Fig. 4.11 Puffed Petal Flower appliqué with button center.

Machine Setup

Stitch length: satin-stitch length
Stitch width: 2½–3
Feed dogs: up
Presser foot: appliqué
Upper tension: looser than normal

Lower tension: normal
Needle size: #70 (10)
Top thread: rayon
Bobbin: regular
Hoop: 5"-7" spring
Stabilizer: Do-Sew or Trace-A-Pattern

Supplies

fusible tricot interfacing, ⅛" basting tape, glue stick, ¾" button, scrap of stuffing

1   Make a cardboard or plastic template of the appliqué patterns (Fig. 4.12). Press a tricot

Fig. 4.12 Patterns for the puffed petal flower include a flat appliqué layer (left, solid line) in the background and individually stuffed petals (center, before stuffing; right, with tuck). (Pattern is 75% of actual size.)

interfacing to the wrong side of the appliqué fabric. The interfacing will minimize ravels on the appliqué shapes and stabilize limp fabrics. Draw and cut out the shapes.

2   Notice that the bottom layer of petals will be treated as one piece instead of as individual petals. Glue-stick the bottom layer of petals to the background fabric. Satin-stitch around the appliqué.

3   Cut five individual petals from the rest of the appliqué fabric with tricot interfacing fused to the wrong side. Pin a tuck at the base of each petal and put four small pieces of basting tape on the back of each petal (Fig. 4.13). Attach the lower half of a petal to the flower. Insert some stuffing and attach the top half of the petal. Repeat until you have added all the petals.

Fig. 4.13 The basting tape on the underside of each petal holds the tuck closed.

4   Satin-stitch around each petal so that it looks like each petal overlaps the next one.

5   The flower center you choose for a sweater will determine whether it is elegant or casual. Consider the difference between using a plain ¾" (19mm) button or a fancy one. A single large rhinestone may be stitched in place for the flower center. Rhinestones are usually machine-washable and easy to care for because they don't require metal prongs for attaching. It is a good idea to turn the garment inside out before washing to protect the rhinestones, beadwork, and stitching.

PROJECT: FOLDED BUDS

The method for making folded buds using fabric is similar to the traditional method of folding one or two ribbons (Fig. 4.14). (A double-sided ribbon is best if you want to try using ribbons.) These little fabric buds are a clever alternative to flat appliqué projects (Fig. 4.15). The fabric for the bud may be cut with the fold on-grain or on the bias. Cutting on the bias will give softer folds, while those cut on-grain will have a crisp finish. Woven fabrics are fine, but lightweight knits won't ravel, and you will need only a straight stitch instead of a satin stitch on the edging of the leaves and calyx.

Supplies

appliqué fabric, glue stick, stamen, straight pins

1 Make the stamen by knotting multiple strands of thread as shown in Figure 7.21.

2 Cut the bud shapes shown in Figure 4.16 from a light- to medium-weight fabric.

3 Fold lengthwise and put two pins near the fold. Glue-stick the lower half, matching the edges. Put the bud on the background fabric and sew through all the layers to attach the stamen. The stitching is ¾″ (19mm) up from the bottom so it won't show when the flower is folded. Use a darning foot.

Fig. 4.14 Original version of the Folded Bud using one or two ribbons.

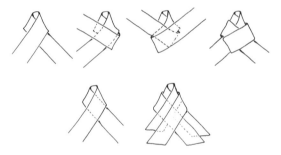

Fig. 4.15 Folded Bud appliqué with thread stamen on a moire lingerie bag.

Fig. 4.16 Folding method and pattern for the Folded Bud.

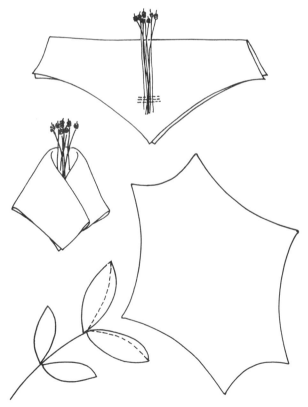

4 Fold the sides as shown and glue-stick in place. Trim all the layers even. Stitch through all the layers on the bottom edge with a straight stitch close to the edge. The raw edges will be covered with a leaf on each side, forming the calyx.

5 Put the leaves in position with glue stick. Straight-stitch around all the raw edges. Satin-stitch or use a decorative machine stitch to finish the edges that ravel.

PROJECT: ROUND-ABOUT FLOWER

Supplies

five or ten 3″ circles of fabric for petals, yarn for English loom flower center

Circles of fabric are used for the Round-About Flower where only five to ten petals are needed. For a simple version, cut five circles at least 3″ (76mm) in diameter. Fold each circle in half and gather each petal along the cut edges. Finish by either folding each piece left over right or meeting the two sides in the

middle (Fig. 4.17). The petals can be sewn directly to either a garment or a background fabric or, if you want to attach the flowers to a project or gift later, sew them to any hooped background fabric. Trim the excess background next to the stitching. For a fuller flower, layer additional petals in several rows. Appliqué a circle of fabric in the center of the flower to cover the raw edges of the petals. Use a medium zigzag or blind-hem stitch so the stitching isn't so noticeable. Use one of the English Loom Flowers from Chapter 5 for the center (Fig. 4.18).

Fig. 4.17 Folding and gathering method for Round-About Flowers.

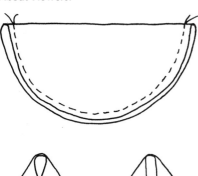

Fig. 4.18 Round-About Flowers with English Loom Flower centers.

PROJECT: RIBBON FLOWERS

Glorious ribbon flowers delicately grace fabric with loops of petals and leaves. Ribbons may be folded, looped, twisted, or knotted before they are stitched in place by sewing machine. Ribbon flowers can be shown off in many ways. Make yourself a bouquet that is suitable for framing (Fig. 4.19). Stitch a bouquet of ribbon flowers on fabric to cover a barrette or adorn the neckline of your favorite sweater with blossoms. I have been inspired by Candace Kling's antique ribbon folding and decided to devise a way to do similar flowers using a sewing machine. Her vast knowledge of the history of ribbon flowers and their uses assures me that these modern creations are as special as the antique ones.

Fig. 4.19 Ribbon Flowers sewn to fabric background using an assortment of ribbon widths and styles.

When ribbon embroidery is done by hand, the ribbons may be threaded through a tapestry needle with a large eye and blunt point, a chenille needle with a large eye and sharp point, or a crewel needle with a long eye. Using soft, narrow ribbons, make the flowers by stitching the ribbon into the fabric, and, if necessary, securing it in place with a second needle and embroidery thread.

Combinations of textures in pliable ribbons can make an exciting piece. Satin, nylon, silk, polyester, and velvet ribbons are wonderful together. Chenille and suedelike cording complement these textures with a soft, napped finish. Cross-stitch and needlecraft stores carry interesting threads like these and more.

You can couch the ribbon to the fabric using machine stitchery instead of sewing it by hand as seen in the color pages. Ribbon flowers can be enhanced with the beadwork and Brazilian embroidery techniques described in Chapter 5. Set up your machine for free-motion embroidery as follows:

Machine Setup

Stitch length: 0
Stitch width: 0
Feed dogs: down or covered
Presser foot: none
Upper tension: looser than normal
Lower tension: normal
Needle size: #70 (10)
Top thread: monofilament
Bobbin thread: regular
Hoop: 5" (127mm) to 7" (178mm) spring
Stabilizer: see Chapter 1

Supplies

2" straight pin, #5 or #8 green pearl cotton, glue stick

Ribbon

4 yds (⅛" wide) for daisies; 1 yd. (⅛" wide) for pin roses; 30" and 20" (1-½" wide) for

wired edge roses; 2 yds. (¼″ wide) for cluster blooms; ½ yd. each (⅝″ and 1″ wide) for green leaves; ½ yd. (½″ wide) for buds

Use monofilament on top and regular bobbin thread below. Prepare your fabric or garment for hooping, as described in Chapter 2.

For best results, cut synthetic ribbons to the desired length and seal the edges with a soldering iron. The petals can be shortened or lengthened to achieve different flowers and textures. Individual ribbon petals can be sewn to fabric, glued to a project, or wired together as a florist would assemble a flower. Layers of ribbon can be secured by poking through all the compressed layers using a soldering iron with a needle point. When the hole is made, the layers fuse together as they melt. This is a basting technique instead of using a stitch.

If you ever find that you will be reeling off yards of ribbon from a spool before or while you are sewing, here are some tips to prevent the ribbon from twisting. Press a pushpin into a nearby surface or piece of wood that the spool sits on. Unwind the ribbon, letting the spool spin freely (Fig. 4.20). This idea works for nearly any spool of ribbon. Or, unwind the ribbon by putting a pencil into the center hole of the spool and letting it free-wheel.

Fig. 4.20 Use a pushpin in the center of a ribbon spool so the ribbon won't twist when it is reeled off.

Pin Roses. Using a narrow ⅛″ wide (3.2mm) ribbon, tie a double-wrapped knot, as shown in Figure 7.20, 1″ (25mm) from the end. It is a simple overhand knot where one of the ends wraps over the other one twice. Machine-stitch it to the fabric at the flower center by sewing around the knot. Insert a 2″

(51mm) straight pin as shown, catching the ribbon and the fabric under the knot (Fig. 4.21). Twist the ribbon as you wrap it around the knot and under the pin until you reach the desired diameter. Pull the end snug, under the pin, and carefully stitch across the rows with monofilament thread next to the pin. Remove the straight pin and your pin rose is finished.

Fig. 4.21 Pin roses (75% of actual size).

Wired-edge Rosette. This technique works best using fine wired-edge ribbons, which are known for their exquisite color gradations and the hairlike wire that encloses both edges. These will serve as the gathering cord on one edge while shaping the flower on the other (Fig. 4.22). This technique is not recommended for machine-washed items because of the wired edges. Any width of ribbon can be used for these flowers. The length will determine whether you are making a bud, a new bloom, or a fully opened flower.

Fig. 4.22 Wired-edge rosettes (75% of actual size).

Because of the fine wire, use a pair of craft or paper scissors to cut the ribbon. This is a good time to use a soldering iron on both edges to prevent raveling. Cut a 3″-length

(76mm) of ribbon and gather it by pulling the wire on one of the edges. The amount of fullness in relation to the width of the ribbon will determine the stage of bloom of the first flower. Next, cut longer or shorter lengths to make one of the other two stages of bloom. A fully opened flower usually requires a length that is at least six times the width. For example, a 1-½″-width (38mm) ribbon should be cut 9″ (229mm) or longer. The new bloom and bud will use half as much ribbon.

Make blooms by gathering one edge of the ribbon, folding both ends under, and rolling the bottom edge. The base of these flowers is flat so that it can be stitched in place with free-motion embroidery and monofilament thread. You may build up the stitching using green rayon or couch pearl cotton to create the calyx. Or you can cover the base by stitching loops of narrow green ribbon. A small piece of Ultrasuede stitched over the base could also make a calyx.

Lazy-daisy Variations. I chose this traditional name for this technique even though it is adapted for stitching on the sewing machine. There are two ways to make the daisies. Choose the one you prefer. You will need about ten petals to make a 1½″-diameter (38mm) daisy with ⅛″ (3.2mm) ribbon. Once you learn how to make a single petal and how to proceed to the next one, you can use either technique for creating leaves or even a stalk of wheat made of narrow ribbon loops.

Use monofilament through the machine needle and set a 0 length/0 width. Secure one end of the ¹⁄₁₆″ (1.6mm) to ⅛″ (3.2mm) ribbon at the flower center with stitching. Hold the ribbon aside while you stitch on the fabric to where the tip of the first petal will be. Next, hold the ribbon perpendicular to that stitching while you sew across it to secure the ribbon at the tip of the petal. Let the ribbon twist as you work (Fig. 4.23, left). Stitching only on fabric, go back toward the flower center, hold the ribbon so it will complete the petal at its

Fig. 4.23 (Left) Lazy daisy with petals crossing the center, (middle) lazy daisy with open center, (right) cluster bloom.

base, and stitch. Bring the ribbon across the center to make a petal on the opposite side. The fullness of each loop varies by the amount of slack in the ribbon from the flower center to the tip of the petal. As the center of the flower becomes thicker, it may be too difficult to sew through. Stitch some of the loops slightly off-center. Or glue a floret from Chapter 7 on top for a center.

Another way to make the lazy daisy is to stitch the loops in sequence, one after another. This variation leaves the center open, with the background showing. A center isn't necessary but can easily be sewn in this opening (Fig. 4.23, middle).

You can manipulate the ribbon in other ways when making a simple loop. Try these variations and you can make many kinds of flowers and not just a lazy daisy.

- stitch loops of knotted ribbon where the knot is on the tip of each loop
- twist the ribbon once for each loop
- overlap rows of loops
- vary the sizes of loops in a single flower
- combine assorted ribbons in a single flower

Cluster Bloom. Once you become skilled with the lazy-daisy variations, you can stitch the dimensional cluster bloom, where only the base of each petal is secured with stitching (Fig. 4.23, right). You will also be working with a continuous length of narrow ribbon instead of with individual ribbon petals. Using a very soft ribbon will give elegant results. The cluster bloom may have uniform loops, loops of varied lengths, or loops with knots on the ends. For any version, anchor the ribbon at the flower center. Begin by stitching loops in the center and add more around them to make a fully opened flower. It isn't necessary to spiral around the center, but, instead, fill in as needed.

Cockades, Cocardes, and Formal Rosettes. These kinds of ribbon flowers were used as military decoration in the time of the French emperor Napoleon. They have surfaced many times since in millinery creations, especially in the 1930s. The folded or pleated petals add an air of formality. Gathering is kept to a minimum. The rosettes may take on a feminine look when applied to a sweater using satin ribbon and a fancy flower center.

Petals can be folded in several ways, sometimes showing both sides of the ribbon. Cut 3" (76mm) to 5" (127mm) lengths of ribbon for the samples. The length depends on the width of the ribbon. Use a 5/8" (16mm) to 1" (25mm) width to start. Fold the petals as shown and glue-stick the two ends together, or use a quick touch with the point of a soldering iron

to fuse the layers of synthetic ribbon until you're ready to sew the ends together.

Put an all-purpose foot on your sewing machine and set a 2 length. Fold 1/4" (6.4mm) accordion pleats lengthwise. Do this either by eye or by using Clotilde's Perfect Pleater (see Supply Sources) for very wide ribbon. Press the base of the petals while they are in the pleater. Straight-stitch the ends of all the loops in a production-sewing fashion, feeding one folded loop after another without cutting the thread (Fig. 4.24). Take this string of ribbon loops from your sewing machine directly to the fabric and glue-stick the petals in place. They may be placed side by side or cut apart for overlapping. Sew them down using a straight stitch across the ends by sewing in a circle (Fig. 4.25).

If the petals are too long, or if a soft ribbon causes the petals to droop, add a straight stitch or decorative machine stitch to hold the loops to the fabric. Sew from the base of the loop toward the end. The tips should remain unattached.

A button makes an appropriate center for this cockade, whether jeweled or covered

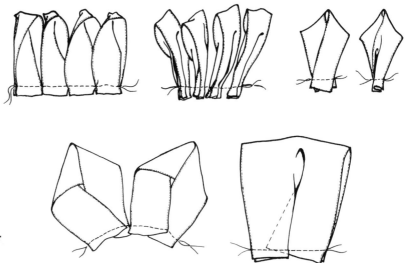

Fig. 4.24 Folding methods for ribbon petals making a cockade.

Fig. 4.25 Assemble the individual ribbon petals into a flower or cockade. Add a button to finish the center.

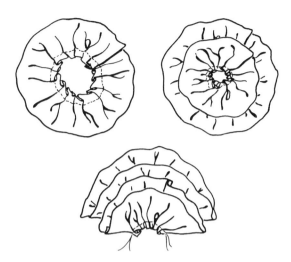

Fig. 4.26 Flowers made from ribbon pleated with a ruffler.

with fabric. The button or other choice of flower center will need to extend over all the ribbon ends. If your cockade has numerous layers of ribbon in the center, most embroidery techniques would be difficult to stitch, so a button is a great solution for a flower center. (See Chapter 7 for more button ideas.)

French Knots. Tie a series of knots close together in a narrow ribbon. They do not have to be tied tightly, just close together. Stitch the ribbon to the background fabric in between the knots, filling the flower center.

Pleated Rosette. This dimensional flower is made from ribbon that has been knife- or side-plaited using the sewing machine with a ruffler attachment (Fig. 4.26)—available from your dealer or by mail-order. A ruffler looks like a complicated mechanical contraption, (see Fig. 1.4), but simply attaches to the presser bar like a darning foot by tightening the thumbscrew and at the same time placing the fork arm over the needle clamp. The ruffler has a setting for #1, #6, and #12, which means that a pleat is made every single, sixth, or twelfth stitch. The ruffles or pleats are not adjustable once they are sewn in.

When the ruffler is set on #1, two yards of ribbon will produce 26" (660mm) of pleated trim to be spiraled on a 2" (51mm) barrette. When set on #6, two yards of ribbon will

produce 42" (1.1m) of pleated trim (Fig. 4.27). The #12 setting will space the pleats too far apart for our purposes.

A firm ribbon such as 1"-wide (25mm) grosgrain will make a beautiful yet durable rosette. Start by pleating two yards of ribbon with the ruffler set on #1 and using a 2 length straight stitch. This setting will make a pleat every time the machine takes a stitch, making a full, ruffly rosette that sews up quickly.

Insert the ribbon into the slot that will guide the right edge so the straight stitching will be ¼" (6.4mm) from the right edge of the ribbon. Don't worry if the pleats aren't spaced evenly; imperfections won't be noticeable when the rosette is formed. To remove the pleated ribbon from the attachment, lift the presser bar and gently pull the work to the back as you would to remove fabric after sewing.

When you are finished, attach the pleated trim to the background with a glue gun by starting at the center and spiraling around. Since it can be made very full, the rosette is perfect for covering barrettes and is especially attractive on home-decorating items (Fig. 4.28).

Fig. 4.27 Pleated ribbon when the pleater is set on (left) #6 and (right) #1.

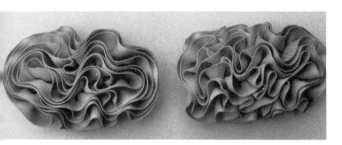

Fig. 4.28 Two pleated rosette barrettes using 1″ grosgrain ribbon. The wavy pattern (left) is made by setting the ruffler on #6. The ruffly pattern (right) is made by setting the ruffler on #1.

To make rosetes on a metal barrette, use a low-temperature glue gun since you will be squeezing the pleats together during the assembly. Start gluing the first row of ribbon ½″ (13mm) shorter on each end of the barrette. Continue to glue and spiral the pleated ribbon around this first row. The first three spirals will be glued to the barrette, and the rest will be glued to each other at the base of the pleats. Use the glue generously to fill areas between the pleats because the ribbon is attached only on its edge. The pleats will lie down as the rosette becomes fuller. Fold and glue the end of the ribbon under to finish (Fig. 4.29).

For a 2″ (51mm) barrette, use a soldering iron to cut a 1-¾″ (44mm) length of 1″ (25mm) ribbon to glue under the arched bar on the back of the barrette. The ribbon will cover most of the gluing area, and it won't ravel since the edges have been heat-sealed.

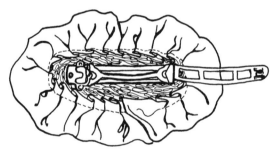

Fig. 4.29 Back of the barrette showing the glued assembly and the last rows of the pleated ribbon.

5

Thread Work on the Sewing Machine

My passion for machine embroidery compels me to share some of the exciting flowers that can be made completely by machine stitchery, composed of an assortment of threads. Some of the flowers in this chapter are stitched directly on fabric. For others, you create the "fabric" with machine stitchery using only embroidery threads.

Couching Novelty Threads and Yarns

Many interesting fibers are too thick to be threaded into the sewing-machine needle and are too heavy for the bobbin. Attach them with machine stitchery by couching them in place using rayon, metallic threads, or monofilament and free-motion embroidery or an automatic stitch. See the color pages, where Bambi Stalder has created the English Loom Flowers by stitching them on a sweater.

PROJECT: ENGLISH LOOM FLOWERS

These loom flowers are 1" (25mm) to 5" (127mm) in diameter and burst open using just about any kind of thread, yarn, or cord. The fibers are wrapped around a circular loom, then machine-stitched around the center, through all the layers (Fig. 5.1).

SELECT A LOOM

The loom for this project can be any ring that is no more than ⅛" (3.2mm) or less thick. For the loom for the smaller flowers you can use

Fig. 5.1 Assortment of rings used for looms and a potted display of English Loom Flowers by Bambi Stalder of Penngrove, California.

a curtain ring, hoop earring, thin bracelet, or metal gasket or washer. I have found 2-½″ (64mm) and 2-⅛″ (54mm) bracelets at children's clothing stores that work well and are as thin as wire. The ridges in the metal hold the threads in place while wrapping. Yarn stores and mail-order sources carry the Susan Bates Pom-Pom Makers. Three sizes of rings wrap nicely and make 2-¼″ (57mm), 1-½″ (38mm), and ¾″ (19mm) loom flowers. Make giant loom flowers with the plastic rings from 5″ (127mm) and 7″ (178mm) spring hoops.

ASSEMBLY

Machine Setup

Stitch length: 0
Stitch width: 0
Feed dogs: down or covered
Presser foot: none, darning foot, or spring needle
Upper tension: looser than normal
Lower tension: normal
Needle size: #70 (10) #80 (12)
Top thread: machine embroidery
Bobbin thread: regular
Hoop: optional

Supplies

assorted threads and yarns, rings for looms, embroidery scissors for snipping

1 Tie the thread or yarn on the ring. Wrap the loom evenly with a novelty yarn or metallic thread, bringing it from one side of the ring to the other (Fig. 5.2). Use just enough tension to keep the yarn from falling off. If you have difficulty with the threads slipping off, coat the ring with rubber cement to make a nonskid surface.

2 Place the wrapped loom on the fabric to be decorated. Stitch around the center of the loom, securing all the wraps by stitching a circle three or four times. If the loom is at least 3″ (76mm) in diameter, use an appliqué foot and a decorative automatic stitch to sew through all the layers.

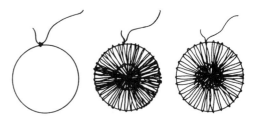

Fig. 5.2 Method of construction for English Loom Flowers. Tie the thread, wrap the loom, and finish with straight or decorative stitching around the center.

3 Clip the yarn all around the edge of the loom so you can remove the flower.

STITCHING IDEAS

- Use an earring for a loom. Open it to remove the flower, sliding off the loops, and it will have petals of loops instead of fringe.
- Using assorted novelty yarns, stitch a cluster of flowers onto fabric used to cover a buckle or large button. This is an easy way to move your creation from a sweater to a belt, hat, or purse.
- Carefully stitch the centers only two times around. Then you can sew the loom flowers directly on the front of a greeting card or gift tag. Too much stitching will weaken the card stock.
- Wrap a metallic thread and yarn at the same time. Make a cluster of flowers using shades of one color in assorted fibers.
- Stitch loom flowers onto water-soluble stabilizer or a tear-away stabilizer so the flowers will stay intact after you sew the centers. They can then be glued to a project individually. Use Japanese Bunka thread or needle punch or Persian yarn so that you can brush some of the flowers to a woolly texture.
- Attach a smaller loom flower on top of a larger one for a flower center (Fig. 5.3A).
- For flowers larger than 3″ (76mm) in diameter, bundle the top layer of threads to make a bud after sewing the center (Fig. 5.3B and

C). If the flower has loops instead of fringe, run a thread through the top layer of loops to gather them together for the flower center or bud.

- Wrap the loom with a thick layer of yarn. Cut the flower off the loom and trim the fringe into distinctive layers.
- Cut the perimeter of the fringe into different shapes instead of just a circle (Fig. 5.3D). (Try a heart, a three- to five-petaled flower, or a star.)

Bobbin Lace Influences

The original idea for lacelike flowers came from my admiration of bobbin lace and the realization that I probably would never be able to make the lace myself. This handwork is almost a lost art, and what you will stitch on the sewing machine will never be identical to it but at least can be inspired by it. These flowers are elegant in their simplicity (Fig. 5.4).

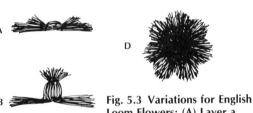

Fig. 5.3 Variations for English Loom Flowers: (A) Layer a small loom flower on top of a larger one. Bundle the (B) fringe or (C) loops to make a bud. (D) Cut the perimeter into shapes.

Fig. 5.4 Lacelike Flowers mounted on tie tacks.

PROJECT: LACELIKE FLOWERS

The stitching for this project is like an open weave and actually creates the fabric from which the flowers are made. Chapter 8 gives complete directions for five methods of stitching thread leaves. Four of these leaves are composed only of thread and one is machine-embroidered on fabric. The leaves are delicate, like the flowers, because they are shaped after all the stitching is complete, leaving only the thread.

PATTERN CHOICES AND REQUIREMENTS

I studied a very old piece of bobbin lace before making my pattern. The cutouts in each petal keep the embroidery light and the de-

sign interesting. Once you have taken care to follow directions for the machine stitchery, make sure not to overwork the petals with excessive stitching. This could destroy the lacelike quality that you want to achieve.

To keep petals separate and to facilitate shaping them later, make each flower by stacking two layers of three petals each. You can easily change the shape of the petal for your own design. Refer to chapter 11 for these changes and for the patterns that can be adapted for lacelike flowers.

Machine Setup

Stitch length: 0
Stitch width: 0
Feed dogs: down or covered

Presser foot: none
Upper tension: normal, balanced with bobbin
Lower tension: normal
Needle size: #70 (10)
Top thread: rayon
Bobbin thread: matching rayon
Hoop: 5" (127mm) spring
Stabilizer: water-soluble

Supplies

transfer method for stabilizer, seed beads, two (3" wide) strips of foil, terry towel, hair dryer, tie tack, craft glue, extra bobbin

EMBROIDERY PROCEDURE

1 Draw two flower patterns on water-soluble stabilizer (Fig. 5.5A). Layer three more pieces of water-soluble stabilizer underneath and put them in a spring hoop with the pattern on top. You can use scraps and irregular pieces for these layers.

2 Stitch on the pattern lines twice. Stitch once in the middle of these lines on each petal. Without cutting your threads, stitch another row on the left and on the right of the

Fig. 5.5 (A) Pattern for Lacelike Flower. (B) Stitching parallel rows inside the petals. (C) Wrap rows of stitching with picot edge. (Patterns are 75% of actual size.)

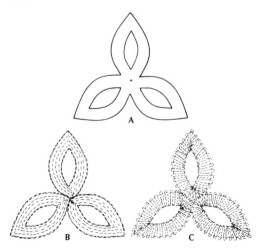

center line. This order of stitching will allow you to stitch a total of three single lines for each petal in parallel rows since the work area is narrow (Fig. 5.5B).

3 Starting at the flower center, stitch across the lines of stitching as if to make warp rows of machine stitching (Fig. 5.5C). These lines secure all the threads together. If your stitching is too dense, the flower will not be lacelike. For each warp line, take one stitch to the outside of the double inner line. Continue back across and stitch a loop composed of three to four stitches beyond the outer edge of the petal. Repeat until all the petals are complete. You can add a few rows of metallic thread on each petal for highlights. When the embroidery is finished, remove the darning foot or spring needle if you used one.

4 Now it is time to bead the petal layers (Fig. 5.6). All the petals will have a few seed beads, but only the top layer will have the center beaded. Use the main flower color in rayon in the top thread and bobbin. Be sure that your beads will slide all the way up the shank of the needle. The seed beads may all be the same size, but the holes are irregular and might cut the thread. Take a few minutes first and try the beads on a spare needle before you start stitching.

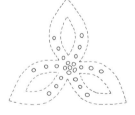

Fig. 5.6 Suggested beading pattern for the top layer of the Lacelike Flower.

5 Secure the threads by taking four tiny stitches in the embroidery. Hold the bead in your left hand and slide it up the needle. Hold it against the needle with your left index finger while turning the handwheel until the needle barely punctures the fabric. If your machine can take one stitch at a time, tap the foot control so the needle will continue down and finish in the raised position. If not, turn the handwheel manually to complete this stitch.

Move the work slightly and turn the handwheel so you will stitch on the side of the bead where you started. Repeat until you have attached the bead with four or five stitches. Since your machine is set for balanced tension, the beads will be attached securely and will roll to one side so the hole is not facing up. The bead cannot roll over if the stitching radiates from the hole, but you could make a decorative effect (Fig. 5.7).

Fig. 5.7 Stitching procedure for attaching beads to fabric with a sewing machine.

SHAPING AND DRYING

Trim the water-soluble stabilizer ¼" (6.4mm) from the embroidery. Soak for five minutes in warm water and massage the stabilizer out of the stitching. The goal is to remove all the visible stabilizer. Some stabilizer will remain in the threads and act as starch as you shape the petals.

Blot the embroidery with a clean terry towel and blot to remove moisture and the stabilizer. Starting at the tips, roll the petals under. Tear a 3"-wide (76mm) strip of foil and wrap it loosely around your finger (Fig. 5.8). Scrunch the edges toward the center to form a doughnut. Make one for each set of petals or leaves to be shaped. This will hold a petal layer while it is drying. Push the center of the flower down into this aluminum-foil doughnut. Air-dry the flowers and leaves on the foil doughnut on a sunny windowsill or, if you are impatient, use a hair dryer.

When both petal layers are dry, glue them

Fig. 5.8 Foil doughnut used for shaping the Lacelike Flower and solid-stitched poinsettia and daisy. Mold the doughnut around your finger.

together with a tacky glue, and use a generous amount to glue a tie tack on the back. These flowers are delicate and can be worn individually or as a pair. They make wonderful earrings, too, if you like something large.

Solid Stitched and Shaded Flowers

The following patterns are designed as an introduction to flower shading with machine embroidery. It is almost like paint-by-numbers and is meant to be a foolproof approach that doesn't require much machine-embroidery experience. These sturdy flowers will hold their shape in splendor. The pattern provided is suitable for a poinsettia (Fig. 5.9) or a Gloriosa daisy. Your choice of rich reds or brilliant yellows will make the difference. (See the color pages.)

Fig. 5.9 Shaded, solid-stitched poinsettia.

PROJECT: POINSETTIA AND DAISY

Study the outline of the flower and leaf cluster. Notice that some petals overlap, while others have small openings near the flower center. Some petals remain separate from their neighbors (Fig. 5.10). All these design features are important, and if you complete the embroidery like these patterns your flower will be lifelike rather than artificial in its symmetry.

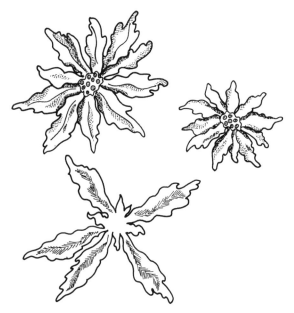

Fig. 5.10 Patterns for the shaded, solid-stitched flowers (50% of actual size).

This project is designed so that a small layer of petals is stacked on top of the larger one, then the flower is placed on top of the leaf layer. The embroidery procedure is basically the same for both petal layers. The only difference is that if you use both layers you need only embroider the flower center on the smaller petal layer. The bottom layer will have the center area filled in with the main flower color since it won't show.

EMBROIDERY PROCEDURE

1   Draw the flower pattern on water-soluble stabilizer and mark one petal with an arrow so you will have a reference point as you work. This way you will know a certain petal on your embroidery is the same one on the pattern.

2   Layer as follows with the first item on top:

water-soluble stabilizer with pattern drawn on it
3 layers of water-soluble stabilizer (use scraps to cover pattern area)
2 layers of tulle in the main flower color

3   Place all the layers into a 5″ (127mm) spring hoop with the pattern on top. If the pattern is too large for the spring hoop, complete the embroidery in sections.

Machine Setup

Stitch: zigzag
Stitch length: 0
Stitch width: 3-½ to 4
Feed dogs: down or covered
Presser foot: none, darning foot, or spring needle
Top tension: slightly loose
Bobbin tension: normal
Needle size: #70 (10)
Top thread: rayon
Bobbin thread: matching rayon
Hoop: 5″ (127mm) spring
Stabilizer: water-soluble

Supplies

transfer method for stabilizer, tulle, extra bobbin, tie tack, craft glue, three (3″ wide) strips of foil, rayon in four shades of flower color, light green, variegated green, and yellow

4   Decide on the color scheme for the

flower (either red or yellow). You will need the shades for the flower petals and the center. The bobbin should be a medium shade (the flower's underside won't show), so you can use assorted colors similar to the main flower color. It's a great way to use up bobbins from past projects.

5 Set the sewing machine to 0 length/0 width and outline each petal twice. Carefully trim the excess tulle. If a petal pulls out of the stitching, hoop another layer of water-soluble stabilizer over the tulle to hold it in place.

6 Set your machine for zigzag using 0 length and 3-½ to 4 width. This technique is known as solid fill-in. Apply a consistent layer of stitching, trying not to build up thick areas, since four colors will be used. Start with the lightest color and fill in each section with the zigzag following the natural grain of the petal. Change the thread to the next shade and stitch in the appropriate sections, overlapping stitching as needed. Repeat with darker shades. Do the last bit of shading with the main flower color. Blend it into the previous shades and finish the edges of each petal to cover the tulle.

I have chosen solid-stitched shaded embroidery using a single needle in the sewing machine. Although you can do the shading with a twin needle, for this pattern a double or twin needle would be clumsy to work with because the petals are narrow. While twin-needle shading will fill in the design faster, you may need several colors for a smoothly shaded project. This technique would require a different approach for applying the colors. However, it is worth considering when using larger patterns as your machine-embroidery skills increase. Use a #1.8 or #2.0 double needle with a medium to wide zigzag, depending on your sewing machine. See Carolynn Baker's article in *Treadleart* magazine (vol. 13, nos. 4 and 5, Jan./Feb. and Mar./Apr. 1991) for projects using this technique (see Supply Sources for address).

FLOWER CENTER

When making a flower with two layers, the detailed embroidery in the center is done only on the top layer of petals. Since you still have the main flower color on your sewing machine, finish filling in the center of the flowers and connect all the petals. This shouldn't be too heavy because the stamen will be embroidered in this area next.

1 Using a 0 length/3-½ width and yellow thread on top, satin-stitch square shapes in different directions with spaces in between (Fig. 5.11, left).

2 Next, use a 0 length/1-½ width to satin stitch a seed stitch on top of each yellow shape with the main flower color. If you pull a loop in the needle thread after stitching each seed stitch, trimming the threads later will be easier (Fig. 5.11, middle).

3 Change the machine setting to 0 length/ 0 width and use a yellow-green thread. Stitch around each yellow shape twice. This will round the corners of the satin-stitched squares. Stitch once with the flower color over the green areas to add contrast and blend the colors (Fig. 5.11, right).

Fig. 5.11 Flower center for the poinsettia or daisy: (Left) Satin-stitch square shapes. (Middle) Satin-stitch a tiny seed stitch on each square. (Right) Outline each square with a running stitch.

LEAVES

Stitch the entire leaf cluster using a spool of variegated green embroidery thread. Another choice would be to select two shades of green and embroider the leaf cluster using 0 length/ 3 to 4 width. Stitch with one shade in the center of the leaves as shown in Fig. 5.10.

Blend the second shade as you complete the leaves.

SHAPING THE FLOWER

Remove the spring hoop and trim the water-soluble stabilizer to ¼" (6.4mm) from the embroidery. Soak the flower in a bowl of hot water for five minutes. Massage the flower edges until the gel from the stabilizer dissolves. Continue to manipulate the flower in the water. Blot the excess on a terry towel.

To shape the petals, roll the tips under and fold them lengthwise with right sides together. You will find the flower will start taking shape and will assume its own personality without much help. Make a doughnut shape from a 3" (76mm) strip of foil as described in Figure 5.8 and use it for drying both flower sizes and leaf cluster.

If the embroidery dries extremely hard, it can become brittle and the petals could break if bent. To correct this, soak the flower again to wash out more of the stabilizer. Reshape and dry. If the flower is too limp, dissolve scraps of water-soluble stabilizer in a bowl of hot water and allow the flower to soak and adsorb the starch. Reshape and dry.

When the dimensional embroidery is completely dry, secure the layers of petals and leaves with craft glue. Mount a tie tack on the back with the same thick craft glue. There are many other options for jewelry findings, such as a stickpin, scarf clip, or even a barrette. Enjoy your creation!

A Study in Hand Embroidery

Hand embroidery is a labor of love, and every stitch is taken with care. Brazilian embroidery offers a contemporary approach, using combinations of traditional stitches in a novel way. Here I have gone a step further and adapted the technique to the sewing machine (Fig. 5.12).

Although there are many stories about its origin, Brazilian embroidery was introduced about 1960 in Rio de Janeiro. This technique is a combination of stitches and knots done by hand with rayon thread. Elisa Hirsch Maia, an avid stitcher, developed techniques and dyed brilliant skeins of rayon thread for this specialty. A Brazilian company, Varicor, produced multicolored rayon threads in several weights that make embroidery easier and brighter.

The popularity of Brazilian embroidery spread throughout South America, and by 1968 it had made its way through Central America, Africa, Australia, Japan, Italy, England, and the United States. Soon this variegated rayon embroidery became known as "Varicor" and, eventually, "Brazilian embroidery." By 1980, the Edmar Company in the United States began manufacturing hand-dyed threads in six weights and in more than 150 color combinations.

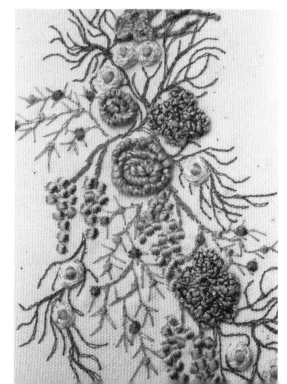

Fig. 5.12 Brazilian embroidery done on the sewing machine by Bette Bland of San Diego.

PROJECT: BRAZILIAN EMBROIDERY

The most popular stitches in Brazilian embroidery make use of the French knot, padded satin stitch, couching stitch, and bullion stitch to create graceful flower sprays as well as birds, fish, and other small creatures. The raised stitches in Brazilian embroidery are distinct from other styles of hand embroidery in that they are worked with a variety of textures in special rayon threads.

I have a keen interest in this style of embroidery and hope you enjoy my adaptations. The sewing machine is not meant to replace, but instead to echo, the texture of representative Brazilian embroidery stitches. See the Brazilian embroidery à *la* sewing machine in the color pages.

CHARACTERISTIC STITCHES

To create the raised stitches by hand, a milliner's needle works best because the rounded eye allows easier threading of the special rayon threads. This needle is good for most of the stitches, such as French knots, feather stitch, stem stitch, and couching. More advanced stitches such as the bullion and cast-ons involve wrapping or actually casting stitches onto a darner's needle because it is longer and has a large eye. There are many stitch combinations, but I include only those that can be adapted to machine stitchery (Fig. 5.13).

SEWING-MACHINE ADAPTATIONS

For Brazilian embroidery on the sewing machine, set up for free-motion embroidery. Hoop the fabric as instructed in Chapter 2. The appropriate needles and thread are noted in the instructions for each technique.

The embroidery will go smoother if you make a cover to prevent the French knots from getting stuck in the holes in the needle plate. The bobbin threads will build up under-

Fig. 5.13 Pattern for Brazilian embroidery (75% of actual size).

neath just as much as the top threads. Cut an index card so that it will cover all the holes and the feed dogs in the needle plate. Make a ¼" (6.4mm) slit with the closed point of small scissors. You will be able to pull the bobbin thread up through this opening and sew any kind of stitch without sewing through the index card. Tape the index card in place.

Regular machine-embroidery rayon or DMC cotton can be used in all the stitchery for stems, twigs, fine growth, and field flowers. The branches, bullion roses, hydrangeas and cast-on blossom can all be made with heavier threads like pearl cotton #3 and #5, Decor #6, or Lola, a Brazilian embroidery thread. These threads can be couched by machine using monofilament on top and a regular bobbin thread below. The stitching will be continuous whenever possible, so there will be fewer places to secure thread tails.

The following stitches are presented in the order in which they should be stitched. The stems, branches, twigs, and field flower buds serve as background for the larger flowers, so do them first. The fine growth may serve as a background or as the final feathery touch, added to soften and balance the composition after the hydrangeas, roses, and blossoms are completed (Fig. 5.14A).

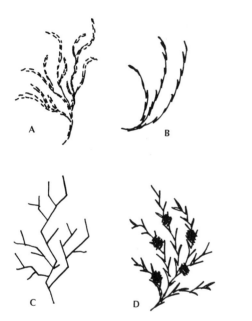

Fig. 5.14 (A) fine growth, (B) stems, (C) branches, (D) twigs with field flower buds.

Supplies
seam sealant

Thread
Three flower colors in #5 pearl cotton, tan in #3 or #5 pearl cotton, green rayon for fine growth, four flower colors in rayon, two tans in rayon for stems and twigs

1 Stems—Not all arrangements include stems, since the twigs, branches, and fine

growth may serve the same purpose. The stem stitch done with the sewing machine follows the same order of stitching as when it is done by hand. Also known as the backstitch, you will progress by overlapping each set of stitches. Turn the handwheel manually to take one stitch forward, take one stitch back, move the hoop and take a stitch forward to accomplish a stemstitch using a 0 length/0 width (Fig. 5.14B). Repeat until the stem reaches the desired length.

2 Branches—These are heavier and more textured than the twigs. First knot a 20" (.51m) length of #3 or #5 pearl cotton about every ½" (13mm). The intervals between knots will not be precise, since you will make each branch individually by stitching the strand in place following the branch pattern. For this couching method, use monofilament in the needle. Cut the pearl cotton next to the stitching after you have anchored the end. A stitch setting of 0 length/0 width will allow you to meander over the branch, stitching the knotted string in place (Fig. 5.14C).

3 Twigs—Make stitches one at a time by manually turning the handwheel on your sewing machine. This takes patience, but you will love this delicate machine stitch, which looks like a feather stitch done by hand (Fig. 5.14D).

4 Field flower buds—A few buds will add a dot of color on some of the twigs when you stitch a 2 width bartack using rayon thread. As you allow the zigzags to pile up, this seed stitch becomes round, like a tiny padded satin stitch. Take four or five stitches before and after each seed stitch to lock the threads in place (Fig. 5.14D).

5 Wisteria—This bloom is made by stitching a series of very small bartacks to make seed stitches (Fig. 5.15, left). Use a 1-½ width; the last few near the tip of the flower are ½ width. Use a rayon ombré and start with the darkest shade in the needle, stitching at the top of the blossoms. As you stitch

Fig. 5.15 (Left) wisteria, (middle) large field flower, (right) hydrangea.

toward the bottom, the lightest color will start to appear. If the ombré changes color suddenly, use a solid-color rayon instead.

6 Large field flower—Although still small, this field flower is an easy one to make in only two steps. First, stitch a padded satin stitch by making a 2 width bartack, then sew a 3 width bartack over it in the opposite direction until you have a round pile of satin stitches. Finish the flower by taking long straight stitches around the center satin stitch with a complementary color until you have an even ring of stitching. This may take about ten rows (Fig. 5.15, middle).

7 Hydrangea—This flower is done with a #5 or #8 pearl cotton on the bobbin to simulate bouclé thread. The fabric is hooped upside down, so you are stitching on the wrong side. Fill in four circular shapes with circle stitching (Fig. 5.15, right). This technique is described further in Chapter 7 as textured bobbin work.

Machine Setup For Hydrangea

Stitch length: 0
Stitch width: 0
Feed dogs: down or covered
Presser foot: none or spring needle
Upper tension: tighter than normal
Lower tension: slightly loose
Needle size: #70 (10)
Top thread: rayon
Bobbin thread: #5 or #8 pearl cotton
Hoop: 7"–8" (178mm–203mm) wooden hoop
Stabilizer: depends on fabric (see Chapter 1)

8 Rose and bud—The Bullion Rose is probably the most noted Brazilian embroidery technique. This stitch may also be used for stalks of wheat. Use a #120 (18) topstitching needle threaded with monofilament, and regular thread in the bobbin. Work with a bundled 1-yard length of heavy thread instead of a whole skein or ball (#5 pearl cotton, Decor #6, or floss). If you run out of thread before finishing the flower, you can add another piece after the last bullion. Starting in the center, take a few small stitches to secure a heavy thread in place. Insert the tip of the needle into the fabric near the last stitch and turn the handwheel until the needle starts to come up, but stop while the needle is still in the fabric. Wrap the heavy thread counterclockwise eight to ten times around the needle. The coil will spring out before you can stitch it in place, so while it is around the needle, apply seam sealant on one side of the coils. The sealant will dry quickly, forming a bullion. With the coils still on the needle, take one stitch. The coils will slide down as a unit as the needle goes up. Anchor the heavy thread after each bullion. You can arch the bullion stitches so they appear as individually stitched petals. Continue to spiral around the center with more bullions (Fig. 5.16, left; 5.17, left).

Unlike handwork, the bullion stitches will spiral one after another instead of overlap-

Fig. 5.16 (Left) Wrapping method on machine needle for bullion stitch. (Right) Wrapping method on machine needle for cast-on stitch.

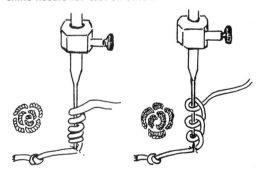

ping. As you progress around the rose, adding larger petals, the stitch will become longer and will require more thread wrapping around the needle, about 10 to 15 times (Fig. 5.17, left). Finish the Bullion Rose by stitching over the tail of heavy thread or by pulling the tail to the backside of the embroidery later. You may want to couch over the bullions with monofilament to hold them in place.

9 Cast-on blossom—Like the bullion stitch, this one is formed by wrapping a heavy thread counterclockwise around a sewing-machine needle but using a half-hitch or by casting on (Fig. 5.16, right; 5.17, right). Use a #70 (10) needle. Seam sealant is helpful to secure the coils. The stitch consists of 10 to 15 half-hitches cast on one side of the needle while it is partially inserted into the fabric. Don't cast these stitches too tight on the needle or you will have difficulty sliding them off when taking a stitch. Take a second stitch near the first one, allowing the cast-ons to slide off and form a loop. The cast-ons may arch if the anchor stitches before and after each coil are close together. If you want it to lie flat, the coils will make a petal shape because of the wrapping method. You will need to secure it by stitching through in a few places with the monofilament thread. A few padded satin stitches as described in Step 6 or couched knots may fill the flower center.

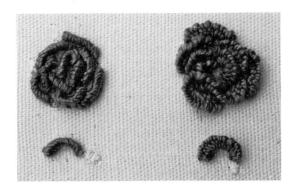

Fig. 5.17 Brazilian embroidery with the sewing machine using the bullion stitch (left) and cast-on stitch (right) to make roses.

10 French knots—These can be represented with seed stitches or done by couching a knotted length of #3 pearl cotton. The thread is sewn in a spiral, stitching across the string in between the knots.

11 Fine growth—These feathery stitches provide the flowing greenery in the background of almost every piece of Brazilian embroidery. The growth may extend from the tips of buds or from stems. The straight stitching goes out and back on each wavy line using a light green rayon thread and a #70 (10) machine needle. This stitching softens the hard, angular lines of bold shapes and colors in the composition.

6

Three-Dimensional Fabric Flowers and Succulents

The four categories of dimensional fabric flowers presented in this chapter are quite different from one another and will appeal to any creative mood. Once you become familiar with each flower, you will be able to create glorious fabric flowers with ease. See the floral arrangements and the Cactus Dish Garden in the color pages.

Three-Dimensional Flowers

All the flowers in this chapter are gathered by machine but are assembled with a threaded hand needle. A few stitches are taken as the fabric is rolled into a flower. When each petal is added separately, the base of the petals is wrapped three times with the thread and secured with more stitching. The method for making these flowers provides sturdy construction while enabling you to manipulate the flower easily and a little at a time. The flower center is attached to the stem wire before the flower is finished.

PROJECT: CABBAGE ROSE

For simplicity, ''cabbage rose'' is the name I give to the most basic fabric flower made from a rolled strip of fabric. As you will see, this flower has many styles and sometimes resembles flowers other than a rose. It gives the illusion of separate petals. The Cabbage Rose is simple to make. Using different combinations of fabrics, patterns, edgings, and methods of gathering will allow you to create many variations (Fig. 6.1). Chapter 3 contains at least ten edging possibilities for you to consider. You can also decide if you want to add color or stiffening to the fabric. Regardless of the type of fabric or method of edging, the cabbage roses will have in common the technique of rolling a strip of fabric or ribbon to form the flower. Variations include using a single layer, a folded strip, or a strip with petal shapes cut on only one edge.

FABRIC CHOICES

Lighter-weight woven fabrics are the easiest to work with. Chiffons, linings, silkies, ruffled lace trim, bridal, and metallic evening fabrics offer exciting results. Sheers with a watercolor-style print create rich, bubbly cabbage roses. Now is a good time to experiment with your samples of painted silk.

Fig. 6.1 Corded basket of Cabbage Rose variations with gathered leaves. Basket by Kitty Wan of San Diego.

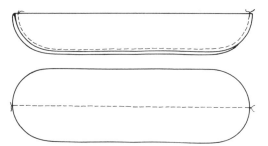

Fig. 6.2 Pattern (75% of actual size) for Cabbage Rose: The pattern length is about four times the width. (Top) Method A, folded in half and the two cut edges gathered together. (Bottom) Method B, with gathering on the center fold.

LAYOUT AND CUTTING

You will be surprised to see the difference in each of the following flowers when you use the same pattern, one cut on-grain and another cut on the bias. Fabric cut on the bias makes softer folds.

Fabrics with a definite right and wrong side are suitable for method A, which uses a strip of fabric folded with the wrong sides together and is gathered on the cut edge (Fig. 6.2, top). Method B, gathered down the center (Fig. 6.2, bottom), is best for sheer, silky, and metallic fabrics because the layers are visible on both sides. This rose strongly resembles a carnation. Cut the pattern piece and apply your choice of edging from the selection in Chapter 3. See the instructions for gathering techniques in Chapter 2, or run a basting stitch with a hand sewing needle. Chapter 8 offers ideas for calyxes.

VARIATIONS WITH METHOD A

A A medium zigzag on the fold (non-gathered edge) of a bias-cut strip of chiffon makes a soft, fluid petal with a fine, crisp edge, much like the swirling skirt of a dancer (Fig. 6.3, center).

B A fabric slightly firmer than chiffon, such as nylon organdy and crystalline, rolls up to make a typical cabbage rose with a soft edge (Fig. 6.3, left, right).

C A delightful flower can be made from a single layer of prepleated fabric. Fold the pattern in half and cut the fabric with the pattern fold on the finished edge of the fabric. The minipleats gather beautifully (Fig. 6.4).

Fig. 6.3 Cabbage Rose variations using different fabrics and flower centers.

Fig. 6.4 Cabbage Rose variation using a single layer of prepleated fabric and a scented center.

PROJECT: DIOR ROSE INSPIRATION

Now that you have tried the Cabbage Rose and realize its diversity when using different fabrics and edges, imagine a flower composed of separate petals instead of one gathered strip. The Dior Rose consists of nine petals—three petals of three sizes; they are traditionally football-shaped with the bias on the length. After folding them lengthwise, gather them on the curved edge, one after another, without cutting the gathering thread. Pull to gather and roll up with the smallest petals in the center.

The following instructions were inspired by the Dior Rose and adapted for the sewing machine (Fig. 6.5). Each petal can be edged with the finish of your choice, gathered individually, then rolled to form the flower. Start with a simple petal design and make three sizes (see patterns Fig. 6.6) with two petals each. You may want to add more petals for larger flowers. Chapter 3 gives directions for the edges that can be used for separate petals. These include machine-stitched techniques and methods of sealing the fabric without stitching.

Fig. 6.5 Arrangement of flowers using petals in graduated sizes and Christmas print fabrics with gathered and padded leaf techniques.

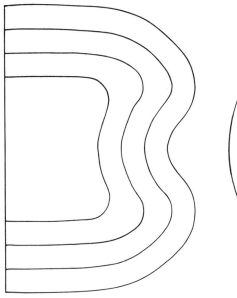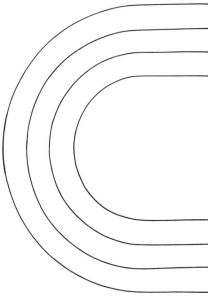

Fig. 6.6 Patterns (50% of actual size) for the two petal shapes used to make the large Christmas-print flowers and buds.

PETAL ASSEMBLY

For a clean, crisp finish on fabrics with a definite wrong side, satin-stitch two layers with the wrong sides glued or fused together. Satin-stitching will also provide the stiffness that a large flower requires. Using two layers of fabric gives you an opportunity to fuse wires in between, to add padding, or to choose a different fabric for the inner and outer petals.

To make petals for flowers larger than 6", bend a cloth-covered wire into the outline of the desired shape. Lay it between the wrong sides of the fabric with a piece of fusible web

next to the wire. The fabric and fusible web should be slightly larger than the shaped wire. Protect the iron and ironing board with a Teflon sheet, then press. After cooling, cut out the petal shape next to the wire. Using an appliqué foot, satin-stitch over the wired edge. Large petals require more wires in the middle of the petal for shaping. They can be satin-stitched on top of the petal later. Stitch beyond the tip of the wire for ⅛" (4.3mm) and build up the satin stitch to match the thickness of the wire. Lock-stitch to finish. This procedure will keep the wire from poking through the stitching.

PROJECT: WILD ROSE

The petals on this flower, rather than being cut on the fold, are cut from two different fabrics. They have a bubbly heart shape when lace is seamed to a piece of sheer crystalline

in a matching color (Fig. 6.7). Draw five petals for each flower on the sheer fabric and layer both fabrics with right sides together (Fig. 6.8). Pin the fabric and sew all the seams

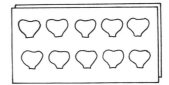

Fig. 6.8 Pattern (75% of actual size) and layout for the Wild Rose petals. Sew through both layers of fabric to make the seams.

Fig. 6.7 Wild Rose with scented centers and gathered leaves in a fabric mâché vase (syrup bottle). Vase by Kitty Wan of San Diego.

⅛" inside the drawn line using an all-purpose foot. Leave the narrow bottom open. Cut out all the petals, then turn them inside out. *Do not* press. Gather the raw edges one after another with a hand sewing needle. Roll into a flower, overlapping the edges. Secure with stitching and wrapping.

PROJECT: NOSEGAY OF LOOPS

The petals for the nosegay are made from fabric tubes, with two layers of loops poised around loop centers. By using numerous loops, the flowers can be made to resemble chrysanthemums, which will add a delicate touch to a bouquet (Fig. 6.9). I will suggest two methods of turning fabric tubes—one with a cord and the other using a unique tool

made specially for the job. The Fasturn tool, made by The Crowning Touch company, works efficiently and allows you to insert stuffing at the same time (Fig. 6.10). The six sizes of Fasturn tools available will make tubes from ⅛" to 1-⅛". The tool comes with an easy reference chart comparing fabric cutting width to cording sizes.

Fig. 6.9 The flowers, leaves, and stems in the Nose-gay of Loops are made from bias tubes.

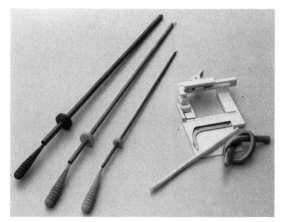

Fig. 6.10 Fastube adjustable attachment (right) for sewing many sizes of tubes and Fasturn tools used for turning fabric tubes in six sizes.

CUTTING AND SEWING FABRIC TUBES

The nosegay flowers are made of short bias tubes 4" (102mm) and 5" (127mm) long. For this reason, cut the fabric into strips, but don't sew them all together in a continuous strip. Strips longer than 25" (635mm) are difficult to turn with Fasturn because of the length of the turning tool.

Work with the strips in a mass-production manner by cutting all the lengths, then sewing them one after another using all-purpose thread and a 2 length.

Select three fabrics for the two styles of flowers. Painted fabric with a soft hand finishes beautifully into narrow loops. Of the two kinds of flowers in the nosegay, the fuller flower consists of eight knotted 4" (102mm) loops surrounded by eight 5" (127mm) wired loops. All the loops are cut 1" (25mm) wide and are turned with the #1 Fasturn tool.

The other flower center consists of four 5" (127mm) loops with a craft cord inside of each one. They are cut 1-1/2" (38mm) wide and are turned with the #3 Fasturn tool. Eight 4" (102mm) loops surround the center and are

cut 1-1/4" wide and turned with the #2 Fasturn tool.

The Crowning Touch company also makes a specialty sewing-machine foot (Fig. 6.10, right) that will sew six tube sizes. I like its design and have found that no matter how careful I am when using an all-purpose foot, the seam is never as good as when I use the Fastube foot for sewing.

Here are a few tips for sewing accurate seams on any size tube with Fastube. Add a 1-1/2" (38mm) square of skid-resistant mesh under the foot platform to keep it from moving. Or tape the front of the foot to keep it stationary. Otherwise the foot will flex when you tug on the fabric while sewing. Pin the seam 3" (76mm) down from the beginning and insert it into the foot. The bias strips will stretch as you sew, keeping the stitching from breaking when you turn the tubes inside out. Insert the fabric and slide the adjustment on the back of the attachment until the cut edges line up with the right side of the foot. This should give you 1/4" (6.4mm) seams.

After making the seams, cut away the selvage edges on the ends of the tubes and trim the seam allowance to ⅛" (3.2mm) before turning the tubes.

TURNING THE TUBES

Without a turning tool, you will need a narrow cotton cord about two yards long, a length that can be used for almost any length of tube. Cut the fabric on the bias and cut one end a little wider. Cutting the top portion of this tube wider will enable you to start the turning more easily. The extra width will be trimmed off later.

Fold the fabric lengthwise, right sides together. Knot one end of the cord and insert it along the fold of the fabric with the knotted end just beyond the top, wider edge. Start sewing across the end of the tube with the knotted cord and sew through the cord. When you begin to sew down the length of the tube, gradually taper the seam until you reach the desired tube width (Fig. 6.11). Trim the seam allowance to ⅛" (3.2mm). Pull the cord at the bottom end until you have completely turned the tube inside out. Cut off the wide end of the tube.

An easier way to make loops is to use the Fasturn tool. When using this tool for the nosegay, I used the three smallest fabric tubes for flowers and leaves.

The fresh, perky shapes of these petal loops are the result of using crisp, synthetic bridal fabrics and heavy, quality cottons. The petal shapes are enhanced by inserting a fine 32-gauge florist wire into the ⅛" (3.2mm) tubes. The widest loops are used for the flower centers. These ⅜" (10mm) tubes are smoothly shaped with a 3.5mm polypropylene craft cord inserted. The same loop and cord are also used for the stems, but a heavy 18-gauge wire is inserted in the center of the cord. The fabric tube holds the cord stable while you work the wire through the center. Bend over ½" (13mm) on the tip of the wire so it will slide through the cord easier (otherwise the sharp end may get stuck in the cord).

Insert the cord into the fabric tube while turning it inside out. Slip the fabric tube over the long end of the Fasturn tool and insert the hook. Before you pull the fabric through the tube, put the beginning of a cord at the end, touching the hook. As you pull the hook, the fabric will draw the cord into the tube at the same time it is being turned inside out. Cut the cord off the skein after inserting it in the tube.

Here are a few tips for successful turning. If the fabric tube will slide onto the metal tube but you discover that it is too thick to slide into it, just hold the fabric snug to the end of the metal tube with the hook and turn it slowly over itself by hand. Also, don't force long lengths of fabric onto the metal tubes. The bias tubes could wrinkle and lose their body. Ironing the tubes would flatten them and aggravate the problem further.

FLOWER ASSEMBLY

Follow these steps for assembling any kind of flower made from bias tubes. It doesn't matter if the tubes have cording or wire inserted. The tightly wrapped base of the flowers fit into a wooden candle cup that serves as the calyx.

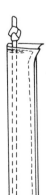

Fig. 6.11 Stitching method for turning any size bias tube inside out using a cord.

1 Start the flower assembly at the center and use a hand sewing needle with a single, long length of thread. Make a loop from the bias tube. Stitch through two ends of the loop ½" (13mm) up from the cut ends. Make tight stitches, then wrap three times with the same thread.

2 Secure the wrapping with several tiny stitches. Use this method to add more loops for the center, then finally surround them with other sizes or colors of loops, making the petals.

3 Finish the base by wrapping and stitching to bundle the base of the loops until they fit into the wooden candle cup. Since the fabric becomes dense and there are wires in the bundle, use wire cutters to chop and trim the bottom of the flower to the desired length.

4 If you use a wooden candle cup for the calyx, the hole on the bottom of the medium cup is perfect for inserting the stem, as illustrated in Fig. 6.12. The smaller cups need the hole drilled larger to accommodate the cord. You might want to stain, paint, or seal the natural color of the wooden calyx to complement your flowers. Add a generous amount of craft glue when the stem is in place. After the glue is dry, coat the inside of the calyx with glue and twist or push the flower into the cup.

5 Finish the end of each stem by cutting the cord and wire 2" (51mm) longer than the

tube so the tube can be tied into a knot and trimmed near the knot.

VARIATIONS

Once you determine the length of the loops, you can make some of the flowers with a knot or bead at the end of each loop. As with other flowers, you can include your choice of a flower center. Consider using a few loops in place of leaves, or use them to add length and drama to an arrangement.

Layer and Stuff

This layer-and-stuff fabric project was inspired by the traditional Christmas tree, in which three layers of tree shapes are seamed, stuffed, stacked, and sewn together down the center. The tree is freestanding, with six sections forming the base (Fig. 6.13). You will enjoy the cactus project, which uses this type of layer-and-stuff technique. Bartack blossoms and stickers stitched on the fabric pieces add interest and realism to these simple shapes. The Suede Minis in Chapter 7 make perfect blooms when they are attached with a glass-head pin for the flower center. Tiny silk flowers look great, too.

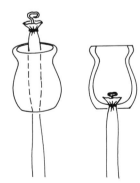

Fig. 6.12 Assembly of calyx using a wooden candle cup and a bias-tube stem with cord and wire inserted.

Fig. 6.13 Traditional layer-and-stuff Christmas tree project.

PROJECT: CACTUS DISH GARDEN

Oh, they look so soft and the fuzzy texture is inviting to touch! If you have made the mistake of gingerly touching a cactus and ended up with stickers in your fingers, you will probably be reluctant to touch these lifelike creations. Felt shapes have never looked so realistic. I took a color photo of three felt cacti to a nursery to have an expert identify one of the creations. He told be that it was generally known as a star cactus since it had six large lobes, but usually with yellow stickers. I couldn't keep a straight face any longer and confessed that these were fabric and artistic license was responsible for the red thread stickers. His expression of disbelief was priceless and a great reward to me. (See the dish gardens in the color pages.)

This garden is landscaped with familiar cactus shapes in felt and single-knit solids (Fig. 6.14). Make this an easy project by using green felt instead of woven fabrics. Rather than sewing and turning all the shapes inside out, leave the seams on the outside.

After sewing the seams, trim the fabric with pinking shears or scallop or wavy-edge shears for a textured edge. A single cactus in a pot makes a clever pin cushion when flower-head pins are pushed into it.

It is fun to see different cactus shapes evolve from the pattern used for felt but using a single knit instead. You can produce still another shape if you stabilize the knit with lightweight fusible interfacing. (A colored netting on the outside also serves as a stabilizer, but not as effectively.)

Manufacturers no longer make wool felt for sewing and crafts because of its expense. Synthetic felts are vivid and luxurious compared to wool and may be either 100 percent polyester or 100 percent acrylic. The Felters Company in South Carolina has been

Fig. 6.14 Cactus Dish Garden made of stuffed felt and single-knit shapes. Constructed by Mary Schaudies of Harlingen, Texas.

manufacturing felt since the early 1900s and, like other companies, has followed the progression from natural fibers to synthetic. They still use wool for industrial felt because gaskets for the automotive trade must contain wool. I prefer acrylic felt because fabric paints and paint sticks blend into the fabric. The felt also accepts glue for craft projects. Polyester felt seems to repel paint and glue, presenting an unexpected challenge.

Supplies

felt in assorted greens; glue stick; red, black, and white tulle; red, yellow, and white all-purpose thread for stickers; pink, yellow, and white rayon for blossoms; white woolly nylon; 32-gauge wire; pinking shears; scrap batting; stuffing; green all-purpose thread; stuffing tool; jar lid for each cactus; gravel; dish; glue gun

CONSTRUCTION

All the cactus patterns and the illustrations of each one assembled are at the end of this chapter. A table, also at the end of this chapter, lists the surface detail variations, seam treatments and shaping techniques (see pages 79 to 82) for each cactus type.

1 Draw the cactus patterns on the right side of the fabric with a washout pen or chalk. Consider using a Sulky iron-on transfer pen since you will need to transfer three to sixteen copies of the same pattern for each plant.

2 Sew the bartack stickers or blossoms on the cactus shapes as described next in Surface Detail Variations. (See below for instructions.) Decide which type of seam treatment you want to use. After you have textured the fabric with stitching, cut out the cactus shapes with a ½" (6.4mm) seam allowance. Layer two sides with wrong sides together and straight-stitch the seams, leaving the bottom open. Use construction thread to match the fabric.

3 Recut the seam to a ¹⁄₁₆" (1.6mm) to ⅛" (3.2mm) allowance, depending on your choice of seam and sticker combination. When using regular straight-edge scissors for trimming, trim each layer of felt and the insert of fabric or thread individually. Use a pair of scissors that has one scooped blade to keep from cutting other layers (Fig. 6.15).

Fig. 6.15 Scissors for trimming seams and threads, especially in difficult areas.

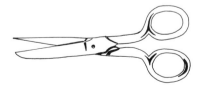

4 Stack three or more of these finished shapes and straight-stitch down the center from the top edge to 1" (25mm) from the bottom edge (Fig. 6.16). This gap will leave room for stuffing each section. The tablike shapes on the bottom of the cactus serve as handles for you to hold onto while stuffing each section. A pair of hemostats is helpful for stuffing. A tool called Stuff-It (see Supply Sources) works well for pushing the fiberfill into small places. You could stuff the shapes first, then sew down the center; but most machines won't like it. And you never want to provoke your sewing machine into a bad mood.

Fig. 6.16 Layer-and-stuff construction of a cactus shape. Stack all seamed shapes and sew down the center through all layers.

5 Trim the excess fabric (tabs) on the bottom of some of the cactus plants. Since each cactus is freestanding, each base is finished by gluing it inside a metal lid from a jar that is about the same size as the base of the cactus. The lids of juice, spice, and baby food jars are the right size for most of the plants. The shorter cacti have a spacer hot-glued between the plant and the lid so the cactus can sit level and not get buried too deep in the gravel. Small blocks of wood or Styrofoam ½" (13mm) thick can work as spacers. The lid will be weighed down as it fills with gravel.

6 Arrange the cacti in a shallow dish and add aquarium rocks or gravel to cover the bases. Why not shed a little light on the subject? Before adding all the gravel, carefully insert clear minilights to make a twinkling dish garden. Arrange them in the gravel so the switch is under a leafy succulent with the button exposed. Cover the wires as you finish filling the rocks. Add tufts of felt to simulate grass. Now you have the absolute easy-care cactus garden, truly drought-resistant!

Because each cactus is designed to stand alone, you can rearrange the garden. The cactus garden can be a decorative source of gifts. On a moment's notice you can "repot" one of the cacti, then add a bow and a card with good wishes.

SURFACE DETAIL VARIATIONS

A If you have a limited color selection of green felt, use fabric markers and paint sticks to color patterns on the fabric or on the edges of the seams. Brush the felt with a wire brush like the one used for Japanese Bunka and needlepunch embroidery. Brushing will raise the fibers to make a woolly surface that softens the impact of the paint or ink that was applied. Blend several colors on the surface of the finished cactus and on the edges of the seams.

B Place a layer of tulle over the felt or single knit before stitching bartack stickers and blossoms or before seaming the fabric shapes together. Experiment with different colors of netting. They change the color of the cactus slightly and the right combination of fabric and net color will give a subtle change. Red, black, and white are effective as single layers or in any combination.

C Cactus stickers can be represented with a pattern of four or five bartacks radiating from a center to make a star (Fig. 6.17, left). Use a 4 width/0 length and stitch about six times for each bartack. On the wrong side of

Fig. 6.17 (Left) Sew four bartacks. (Middle) Snip the top threads to make bartack stickers. (Right) Snip the bobbin threads of the bartacks to make bartack blossoms.

the work, put a dab of craft glue or seam sealant in the center of every star. Snip each bartack on the right side near the tip (Fig. 6.17, middle).

D To make small rayon thread blossoms, stitch a bartack star as in C above, stitching about ten times for each bartack. Put a dab of craft glue or Fray Check in the center of the star on the backside. Cut the bobbin thread near the outer tip of each bartack. Fluff the top threads, releasing them from the bobbin threads. They will rise and have a sheen just like live cactus blossoms (Fig. 6.17, right).

E Sew "two-in-one" bartack blossoms at the same place on each fabric shape before sewing the seams. When the cactus is firmly stuffed, the flowers should touch each other and blend to make a fuller single bloom (Fig. 6.18).

Fig. 6.18 Full bartack blossoms in the seams when the two sides touch and join two flowers.

SEAM TREATMENTS

A Enclose stickers in the seams by inserting strands of polyester thread (Fig. 6.19, left cactus), which stands out better than fine embroidery threads. White, off-white, rust, brick red, and mustard are good colors to use.

Fig. 6.19 In leftmost cactus, thread stickers were inserted in the seams every ¾″ (19mm). In middle cactus, thread stickers are surrounded with woolly nylon. In cactus at right, thread stickers were inserted in the seams between two layers of batting.

Make the sticker bunches by cutting ten lengths of all-purpose thread, each one yard long. Treat them as one cord and tie a single knot at 1″ (25mm) intervals. Cut the strand on one side of every knot. Glue-stick each sticker bunch along the edges of the cactus shape, or simply insert them every ¾″ (19mm) as you sew the seam. The stitching should trap all the knots on the inside. Color the bases of the sticker bunches using fabric markers. After finishing the seam, trim the stickers to a uniform length.

B Some cactus plants have a woolly texture around the stickers. Make this texture by knotting a yard containing ten strands of polyester thread and eight strands of woolly nylon (a serger thread). After sewing the sticker bunches into the seam, pull all the threads even and cut them the same length. The woolly nylon will then shrink close to the base of the polyester stickers (Fig. 6.19, middle cactus).

C You may want to stabilize the single knit by fusing lightweight interfacing to the wrong side. Most likely it will show when the seam is trimmed, so why not color it? Use fabric markers or paint sticks to color a ⅜″ (10mm) border on the interfacing all around each shape. Yellow, orange, green, and brown are good color choices.

D Another way to add color in the seam involves ½″-thick (13mm) batting and sticker bunches (Fig. 6.19, right). Between the two layers of felt, place two ¾″-wide (19mm) strips of batting with a sticker bunch in the middle at regular intervals. Sew the two felt shapes together with the batting and stickers inserted into the seam. Pink all layers to ¼″ (6.4mm), except the polyester sticker bunches, which are longer. Use fabric markers to color the center edge of the batting. Blend a bright color like yellow, orange, or red with a dark color like brown, gray, or green.

E An interesting edge can be achieved by layering a piece of organdy on the wrong side of each piece of cactus fabric (Fig. 6.20). Trim all the layers individually after sewing the seams around the shape. Cut the fabric close

Fig. 6.20 The illusion of fine stickers, made from nylon organdy and inserted in the seams.

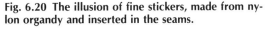

to the stitching, and cut the organdy ⅛″ (3.2mm) to ¼″ (6.4mm) beyond the cactus cut edge. Manipulate the organdy until you have frayed it completely. Use a wire brush for Japanese Bunka and needlepoint embroidery to fray the organdy edge.

F A more complicated—but exciting— seam is just like the previous one but uses two layers of organdy (cut on the bias) with sticker bunches in between (Fig. 6.21, smaller cacti). After enclosing these materials in the seams, trim all the layers individually at different lengths. Cut slowly to avoid cutting the stickers, which extend beyond the organdy.

G To make a solid fuzzy edge, insert a gathered strip of organdy into the seam. Cut the ¾″ (19mm) strip on the bias to prevent loss of thread. Gather it to create a dense amount of organdy that will conform to any shape. Sew the seam, then trim the fabric close to the stitching and cut the organdy to ¼″ (6.4mm) seam. Fray the organdy com-

pletely to the seam. The wire brush allows you to fray quickly (Fig. 6.21, large cactus).

H Insert a second color of felt into the seams for another seam treatment. Place a piece of felt that is larger than the cactus shape between the two pieces to be sewn together. When cut with pinking, scalloping, or wavy-edge shears, the felt makes a clever edge because the middle layer has a wider seam than the cactus shape. To reduce the bulk, trim the center area of the colored insert before sewing the seam.

I I have made an exciting discovery: When using scalloping shears to cut the left edge of fabric shapes, the shears will make the reverse pattern of the normal scallop, as though you have cut the right edge of the fabric as well (Fig. 6.22). Even though I am right-handed and the scalloping shears are designed for the right hand, I can use them comfortably with my left hand. This new cutting edge is a fun application for the cactus garden.

Fig. 6.21 Two layers of nylon organdy with thread stickers in between are inserted into the seams of the two smaller cacti. A ruffled strip of nylon organdy makes a dense row of fine stickers in the seams of the large cactus.

Fig. 6.22 Two different patterns made by using scalloping shears to cut on the left and right side of the blade.

SHAPING

A Some cacti are concave and appear hollow rather than full and are made with very little stuffing (Fig. 6.23). Another way to accomplish this illusion on the main stalk is to sew a second seam ¼″ (6.4mm) to the inside of the first seam. The smaller shapes that attach are not stuffed at all but contain a wire that is 2-½″ (64mm) to 4″ (102mm) long. The wire is not sewn into any of the seams and is almost as long as the shape itself.

B When making a succulent leaf, use a single layer of felt for each layer of leaves.

Fig. 6.24 Sewing method for inserting fine wire in each shape of the leafy succulent.

Fig. 6.23 Three-sided cactus with light stuffing in the main stalk and no stuffing in the wired arms.

Work with a 12″ (305mm) length of 32-gauge florist wire or plastic-coated telephone wire. Fold a single leaf lengthwise with right sides together and glue-stick a wire in the fold, starting in the middle of the leaf layer (Fig. 6.24). Starting in the center, use an edge-stitching foot to sew a very narrow seam just wide enough to encase the wire. The seam starts at the base of each leaf and stops before the pointed tip. It will look like a pintuck on the underside of the leaf. Cut the wire. This procedure will make the sewing proceed like clockwork.

Assemble the plant by stacking all the layers with a ⅜″ (10mm) felt spacer in between each layer. Using scraps of felt, make samples to see how many layers your machine can sew through. Stitch a bartack through the bottom layers of the assembly. Stitch the remaining top layers together, then glue the two stacks together. The bartack, spacers, and pintucks are essential for creating the subtle shaping of this succulent.

C Tiger jaws cactus uses another version of the layer-and-stuff technique with stuffed shapes stacked in opposite directions. The cactus is made up of plantlets that have three layers each. Each pair of leaves uses two pattern 1 pieces seamed (sew side A to A) and joins pattern 1 to pattern 2 with all the seams on the outside (side B to B and side C to C). They are trimmed with pinking shears. Each plantlet is assembled and secured with a bartack. A cluster of plantlets is stitched together by hand to make a cactus.

Below are the cacti and their patterns (Fig. 6.25). The following table lists the surface detail variations, seam treatments, and shaping techniques (described on pages 79 to 82) that are used to make the cacti shown in the photographs. Try the other techniques as you make your own cacti.

TECHNIQUES USED FOR EACH CACTUS TYPE

	Large blue candle	Small blue candle	Succulent rose	Fairy castle	Cande-labra	Barrel cactus	Lobivia	Star cactus	Tiger jaws
Surface detail variations									
A. Fabric painted or colored			●	●	●				
B. Fabric layered with tulle	●	●						●	
C. Cactus stickers on fabric	●	●		●	●			●	
D. Thread blossoms on fabric	●								
E. Two-in-one bartack blossom	●								
Seam treatments									
A. Stickers in seam	●								
B. Stickers with woolly base		●							
C. Single knit with fusible interfacing								●	●
D. Stickers with batting	●								
E. One layer of organdy in seam	●								
F. Stickers between two layers of organdy							●	●	
G. Gathered bias strip of organdy						●			
H. Second color of felt in seam	●	●							
I. Cut edges with scalloping shears backwards	●			●	●			●	
Shaping techniques									
A. Hollow, three-sided branches with wire				●	●				
B. Wire in pintucks			●						
C. Tiger jaws technique									●

Star cactus

Blue candle

B   C
Cut 2
for each
plantlet
C   B

A   A
C   B
Cut 4
for each
plantlet

Center bud

Cut 2 for
each bud

Tiger jaws

Blue candle

Barrel cactus

**Fig. 6.25 Cactus patterns (50% of actual size) and il-
lustrations of the finished shapes.**

Candelabra

Fairy castle

Lobivia

Succulent rose

7

Flower Centers

Many of the flowers in this book are complete without a flower center, but I have dedicated this chapter to making flower centers because there are so many interesting options. By selecting either a subtle or a striking color, you can greatly enhance the presentation of your fabulous fabric flowers. The flower centers described will involve a variety of threads, fabrics, and craft supplies. They even provide a convenient way to add scent and hide the actual construction of some flowers.

Before you jump into new techniques, consider using smaller versions of the fabric flowers in the previous chapters. They can be wired, stitched, or glued into the fabric flowers during the assembly or after the flower is completed. Smaller, single flowers can be used in the center or as a cluster. The flowers that are most appropriate for adding flower centers are the English Loom Flowers in Chapter 5 and the Cabbage Rose variations and fabric loops in Chapter 6.

Florets

Diminutive florets compose a dense cluster that is suitable for a flower center (Fig. 7.1). Like a sunflower's center, filled with hundreds of tiny flowers, you can create your own fantasy blooms using multiples of spiral cones and Suede Minis. Nature sometimes presents fantastic flower centers, and the petals serve as a quiet background for them.

Fig. 7.1 The center of the sunflower is a covered button with ten spiral cones sewn on. Petals are made from Point d'Esprit netting.

PROJECT: SPIRAL CONE CLUSTERS

I have loved the simplicity of these ruffly little flowers ever since I saw one fly out from under the fast stitching needle of Joy Clucas from England. Ten spiral cones compose the centers of the daisies. The magic of this flower's success is based on puckered machine embroidery. In other words, this is a good example of how to take advantage of mistakes. Machine embroidery requires that fabric be held taut in a hoop, and usually you avoid making short, tight stitches. Let's break the rules.

Supplies

synthetic sheers, rayon to match, extra bobbin for each color, stamen, all-purpose thread if wrapping by hand

Place a sheer synthetic fabric into a 5" (127mm) spring hoop. Nylon organdy, crystal organdy, and chiffons are ideal for this technique. Loosen the fabric in the hoop a little by pushing your thumbs in the center. Using a darning foot or spring needle is optional. Stitch a spiral, starting in the center, with all the rows very close together (Fig. 7.2A). The machine speed is medium to fast and the stitches are as short as possible—about 1-½ length or 15 stitches per inch.

The floret finishes about ¾" (19mm) in diameter, and each one is stitched two to three times on the last row of stitching. If your spiral becomes irregular, don't fight it. Exaggerate the pattern until it starts to resemble a flower shape. Make leaves simply by stitching the outline of two or three leaves in a cluster and continue stitching a spiral to each center. A plain fabric leaf without spiral stitching is a good addition to the spiral cone florets. Finish

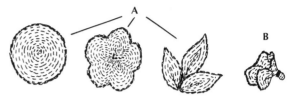

Fig. 7.2 (A) Patterns for making spiral cone florets and leaves. (B) Method of stitching spiral cones to fabric background.

all the flower shapes by stitching three times on the last row. Use a soldering iron instead of scissors to cut out the florets. (See Chapter 3 for detailed information on using a soldering iron.) Sizzling the edge can be done quickly and seals the fabric whiskers to prevent raveling.

Shape the spiral cones by pushing the center out with your thumb or by pulling the shape over the eraser end of a pencil. Now you have spiral cones. To attach each floret to fabric, bundle the cut edge in your left hand and stitch by machine across the other end, which is the floret's center (Fig. 7.2B). After stitching a few florets in place on the background fabric, they will hold one another upright and the bottoms will not show. A piece of fabric covered with these florets can be used to cover a barrette or a button for jewelry. If the centers of the florets are individually wrapped with thread instead of being stitched to fabric, they can be glued to any surface instead of being attached with machine stitching. You can also add thread loops or other stamen so the wrapping will hold it in the floret.

PROJECT: SUEDE MINIS

These diminutive flowers are lively bursts of color (Fig. 7.3). The only machine sewing necessary is done to attach the florets to the fabric. The secret to the success of the Suede Minis is that they are made from a nonraveling fabric that allows detailed cutting. Small scraps of synthetic suedes are best. (See the garland in the color pages.)

Fabrics with similar characteristics, such as felt, will work for some of the Suede Minis, but the strength, stretch, and thickness of Ultrasuede are critical for others. Facile, Caress, and Ultraleather are high-quality fabrics that also may be used. They will have varied results because the weight of the fabrics differs. This is a good project on which to use Sulky iron-on transfer pens to transfer cutting lines and shading. Since the line will show, use a pen color similar to the color of the flower. On Ultrasuede, iron the transfer on the wrong side.

Ultrasuede petals can be colored with

Delta/Shiva Paintstiks, giving fantastic results (see Chapter 3). Add any detailed stitching to the painted fabric before cutting out the shapes so that you can hoop the fabric while sewing. You can add stitching details to cut shapes placed between two layers of water-soluble stabilizer and put into a spring hoop. After finishing the stitching, cut away the large pieces of stabilizer and dissolve the rest in a bowl of hot water.

The florets are designed as a single layer of petals, but you can also combine layers of different sizes or patterns to make a single flower (Figs. 7.4 through 7.13). When sewing the flower to the background fabric, add a seed bead for the center. The bartack stars used for cactus stickers and blossoms in Chapter 6 also make tiny centers for Suede Minis. The stitching done to make these centers also secures the flower to the background. Beading or decorative stitching should be done only on the top layer if you plan to use several layers for one flower. Sew them all together with a #70 (10) needle and a darning foot.

Group the florets close together so thay will hold each other upright. This is the simplest way to make these cutouts three-dimensional. I have designed some of the Suede Minis (such as the Mother's Flip and Double Leaf) to hold their shape by passing the petals or leaves through a slit at the petal's or leaf's own base. With only $1/16$" (1.6mm) to $1/8$" (3.2mm) of fabric between the slit and edge of the petal, Ultrasuede is tough enough to withstand the tugging needed for this technique.

There are many other tricks to make a flat flower come alive. Try the three-dimensional techniques used with silk flowers in Chapter 4. Lift the petals and leaves so they arch, then tack the tips to the fabric. Let them twist and overlap. The goal is to make an interesting flower, not a perfectly symmetrical one.

Fig. 7.3 Suede Minis assembled into a brooch that can also serve as a scarf pin.

Suede Minis can also be made with wire stems for use in arrangements. String small beads on one end of a wire and twist to form the flower center. Poke a hole in the flower with an awl and slide the flower onto the stem. The posy, carnation, and dahlia are shaped by wrapping with all-purpose thread. Wrap tightly around the flower, with the thread placed in between the petals. Tie a square knot on the bottom to secure. This wrapping will shape the flower by gathering and cupping the petals. Pinwheels, lilies, and forget-me-nots are flowers that need to be sewn and can be stitched on top of a hooped piece of water-soluble stabilizer. Tear away the stabilizer after finishing the sewing. For all flowers except the lily, slide a bead up the wire to serve as the calyx. Add a drop of craft glue between the bead and back of the flower.

Suede Minis' leaves can easily be attached to a wire stem. Fuse a cloth-covered floral wire to the underside of each leaf by placing a 1/8"-wide (3.2mm) piece of fusible web between the Ultrasuede and wire. Cover with a Teflon sheet and press. Cover the fused side with a wet press cloth and press a second time. When completely cooled, peel the leaf from the sheet. The fusible web shrinks during fusing to surround the wire, forming a strong bond, and will hardly be visible. Each of the Suede Minis is illustrated with its pattern below.

Supplies

Ultrasuede scraps, paintsticks, scissors for detailed cutting, transfer method, all-purpose thread to match for wrapping by hand, pinking shears, glue stick

CONSTRUCTION

Forget-me-not. Each flower consists of two pattern shapes. Take one set and twist it tightly twice so the right sides face up (Fig.

7.4). Sew across the twisted center two times with a straight stitch. Twist the other set, place it across the first set, and sew across it to secure. The petals will lift and twist into shape. If you want to put this flower on a wire stem, do the sewing on a piece of water-soluble stabilizer. Remove the stabilizer and glue or wrap a wire to the flower.

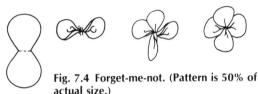

Fig. 7.4 Forget-me-not. (Pattern is 50% of actual size.)

Posy. Cut slits between the three petals toward the center of the flower until they are only 1/8" (3.2mm) apart. Wrap a construction thread tightly around the flower. The thread wrapping will draw the petals up before the flower is stitched in place (Fig. 7.5).

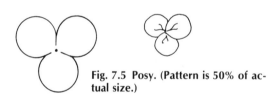

Fig. 7.5 Posy. (Pattern is 50% of actual size.)

Lily. A single yellow pistil is surrounded by the white petal. Place the pistil on top of the petal and fold one side over the other. Sew across the base to secure (Fig. 7.6).

Fig. 7.6 Lily. (Pattern is 50% of actual size.)

Carnation. This flower has eight sections that are cut toward the center until the slits are ⅛" (3.2mm) apart (Fig. 7.7). The outer edge may be cut with regular scissors for a plain edge or with pinking or wavy-edge shears. Shape the flower by wrapping construction thread between the slits like the posy, then slit the outer petal edges to make the fringe effect.

Pinwheel. Make each flower using three sets of the "Z" pattern (Fig. 7.8). With the right side facing up, fold the ends to the center line. Glue-stick and sew with a small zigzag to secure. Stack three sets, spacing the petals evenly, and bartack to hold.

Mother's Flip. Use one or more of these petal layers to make a flower. Form the dimensional petals by passing the tip of each petal into the slit at its base with the right side up (Fig. 7.9). Stacking multiple layers will

cause the petals to point upward. The only sewing needed is to add the flower center or secure multiple layers.

Dahlia. Assemble this six-petaled flower the same way as the posy and carnation by cutting the slits between the petals until they are ⅛" (3.2mm) apart near the flower center and wrapping with construction thread (Fig. 7.10). The cutout in each petal is done with a leather punch to keep the size consistent.

Wavy-edge Leaf. Cut out these almond-shaped leaves using pinking, wavy-edge, or scalloping shears (Fig. 7.11). Sew the leaf to the background fabric or fuse a wire to the underside.

Split Leaf. The design of this leaf makes it dimensional when you overlap the two points, creating the base of the leaf. Sew across the

Fig. 7.7 Carnation. (Pattern is 50% of actual size.)

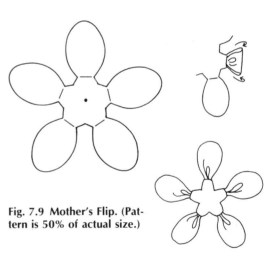

Fig. 7.9 Mother's Flip. (Pattern is 50% of actual size.)

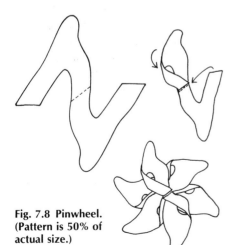

Fig. 7.8 Pinwheel. (Pattern is 50% of actual size.)

Fig. 7.10 Dahlia. (Pattern is 50% of actual size.)

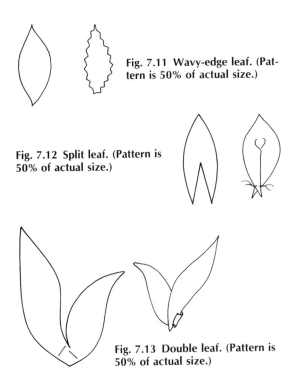

Fig. 7.11 Wavy-edge leaf. (Pattern is 50% of actual size.)

Fig. 7.12 Split leaf. (Pattern is 50% of actual size.)

Fig. 7.13 Double leaf. (Pattern is 50% of actual size.)

points with the leaf on the fabric or by itself so it can be glued to a project (Fig. 7.12).

Double Leaf. This pair of leaves becomes gracefully three-dimensional when you pass the tip of each leaf into a slit at the base (Fig. 7.13). Each leaf can go into its own slit or cross over into the opposite side, making the pair more dimensional. The only sewing needed is to attach them to fabric.

Embroidery on Covered Buttons

Your sewing machine is capable of producing interesting textures that will make a variety of flower centers. The centers are stitched on fabric and the fabric is used to cover buttons or a padded disc. Usually covered buttons are available in fabric stores in sizes ranging from ⅜″ (10mm) to ⅞″ (22mm). See Supply Sources

for suppliers of unusually large covered buttons. Also check your local needlecraft or cross-stitch stores for round or heart-shaped buttons and oval or rectangular barrettes that assemble like covered buttons. These large buttons are perfect backings for embroidered flower centers.

Determine the amount of fabric needed to cover the button or barrette that you will use for the flower center. If you intend to cover the button or barrette with fabric as the directions indicate, remember to go easy with the stitching as it nears the edge of the button. From experience, you know how difficult it can be to work all the fabric into the back of a covered buton. The petals will probably cover the edge of the button as they cup around it.

There are two types of buttons, both finishing with a back that snaps on. One has teeth to grip the fabric, while the other uses a plastic tool to force the fabric into place. When using either button, stitch a basting stitch ⅛″ (3.2mm) from the cut edge of the fabric. Apply glue stick on the fabric that will contact the top of the button. Press the button in place and draw up the basting stitch, gathering the fabric to fit snugly. Secure with a knot. Adjust the fabric to align the stitching, then pop the back on the button. You won't need any special tools for this method and the fabric will always line up perfectly.

A simple texture for covering a button involves couching a strand of knotted yarn to the fabric. Knotted yarn is a series of knots less than ¼″ (6.4mm) apart. This spacing allows for twisting and overlapping the yarn as you stitch it in place and fill the area with the desired density of knots (Fig. 7.14, top left). Sometimes a combination of threads or fine yarns will yield a rich and unusual texture. Try a few of the Brazilian embroidery techniques from Chapter 5 for stitching flower centers.

This couching technique gives best results if

you use monofilament thread in the needle and regular machine-embroidery thread in the bobbin. The clear monofilament is barely visible when stitched over light or medium colors. Gray or smoke-colored monofilament blends perfectly with darker colors. Using a darning foot will help control the work, but this won't be necessary once your skill in maneuvering the yarn increases. The stitching is meant to anchor the yarn before and after each knot, so stitching around each knot is sufficient.

Have you been saving thread scraps for who knows what reason? While you are still warmed up to the idea of stitching fibers down to create a texture on the surface of the fabric, let's try a great idea for emptying spools and bobbins. Now you can reel off the threads from your bobbins and nearly empty spools. Cut up the threads over the fabric onto a circle drawn the size of the flower center. Stop when the area is full. Use a running stitch and sew over all the threads with random straight stitching. Leave the edge shaggy or trim it after covering the button (Fig. 7.14, top row, middle).

Fig. 7.14 Embroidery on covered buttons showing (top row, left to right) couched knots, stitched chopped threads, use of the fringe foot, and (bottom row, left to right) stitched thread loops, textured bobbin work, and ruching.

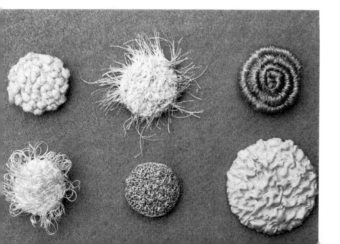

FRINGE FOOT OR TAILOR'S TACK FOOT

Experiment with a fringe foot or tailor's tack foot on your sewing machine. The foot has a raised bar in the center, and you must use a wide zigzag with it. The top thread will stand as loops on the surface of the fabric. Try threading two threads of different colors through a #80 (12) or #90 (14) needle. Multicolor and metallic threads will add even more interest.

The principle of this technique is to stitch loops very close together in parallel rows to fill an area with texture (Fig. 7.14, top right). This is accomplished by sewing a satin stitch in a spiral pattern; being careful not to stitch into previous rows of loops. The fringe foot attachment can help you sew a thick, plush flower center of loops. Start with a 4 width and a satin-stitch length of about ½. After the first spiral, change to a shorter length so the stitching will continue with good density. Finish by cutting the top thread on the take-up lever on the sewing machine. Slowly slide the last loops off the foot and insert a large plastic yarn needle in them as you remove the work from the machine. This will keep the loops from pulling flat before the bobbin thread is cut. Tie off on the back side and use seam sealant on the knot. This method was used on the centers of the gingham flowers on the straw hat pictured in the color pages.

THREAD LOOPS

Another way to make a clustered flower center is to stitch loops using the top thread (Fig. 7.14, bottom left). Make sure the presser bar is down. Take a few stitches to lock the threads in place. Slowly pull thread slack from the needle. Hold a ¼" (6.4mm) loop down to the fabric with a small hand tool like a screwdriver, seam ripper, or tweezers. Take a few stitches across the base of the loop to secure it. Pull another loop and stitch it in place. Repeat until you have filled the flower center with the desired number of loops.

TEXTURED BOBBIN WORK

You will find many names for the texture I will simply call "bobbin work" (Fig. 7.14, bottom row, middle). They include moss stitch and Russian stitch. Bobbin work bears a resemblance to needle-punch embroidery, which is done with a special hand tool. Many machine-embroidery enthusiasts will refer to this same technique as couching. I feel this term is inaccurate because couching is traditionally worked by hand on the right side of the fabric, stitching a heavy thread to the fabric with a fine thread. Here, heavier threads, cords, and ribbons are stitched or couched to the fabric using the sewing machine instead of a hand needle. With a sewing machine, bobbin work consists of using a thread in the bobbin that is too thick to thread through the needle. The machine embroidery is done on the wrong side of the fabric to accommodate the threads, with a tighter top tension.

Although you can use many different kinds of threads, such as fine yarn, floss, and knitting ribbons, it will be safest to try a common thread. DMC pearl cotton comes in sizes #3, #5, and #8 (heaviest to lightest). Use #8, since you will be able to wind more of it on the bobbin. The top thread can be rayon, metallic, or even all-purpose thread. The top thread can match the color of the pearl cotton, or use a contrasting color. This same machine setup is used for the hydrangeas in Chapter 5.

Machine Setup

Stitch length: 0
Stitch width: 0
Feed dogs: down or covered
Presser foot: none or spring needle
Upper tension: tighter than normal
Lower tension: slightly loose
Needle size: #70 (10)
Top thread: rayon
Bobbin thread: #5 or #8 pearl cotton
Hoop: 3" (76mm) to 5" (127mm) spring

Think of this technique as reverse-tension embroidery. In other words, you will be sewing on the wrong side of the fabric. Wind the bobbin with the heavy thread. You may need to hold the ball of thread on a pencil in an upright position while filling the bobbin. Winding by hand may cause the thread to twist in the wrong direction as it comes off the bobbin.

Depending on your machine, there are a few different ways to insert the bobbin to give you the loose bobbin tension needed for the best results. If your bobbin drops into the machine and has a bypass opening that avoids the tension spring, bring the thread through this opening. For an even looser tension, insert the bobbin upside down and thread it through the bypass opening. This type of machine might allow you to change the bobbin tension easily, so experiment with lower tensions before using the bypass. This will give you a more precise and controlled stitch, while the bypass will produce a soft, looped stitch.

If your machine uses a bobbin case, the case may have an opening that avoids the tension spring. There may also be a hole in the bobbin case lever so you can add a slight tension when you pass the thread through it after the opening.

The other option is to loosen the tension spring on the bobbin case. If the bobbin case has two screws, the one closest to the tension finger adjusts the tension. The other screw fastens the tension finger to the bobbin case. Loosen it in quarter-turns, and be careful not to overdo it since the screw is extremely short and difficult to screw back in. Hold the bobbin case over a piece of fabric in case the screw falls out. Then you won't have to search for it on the floor.

Ideally, you may want to purchase a second bobbin case and adjust it for use only with pearl cotton and keep your original bobbin case for regular sewing and embroidery. Before you start tinkering with the tension in the bobbin case, try turning the bobbin upside down so the thread will unwind in the opposite direction to the way it normally would. This allows very little tension on the bobbin, and you should stitch carefully until you see that your sewing machine is agreeable to this setup.

Since you are using embroidery thread on top, use a #80 (12) needle. The top tension should be tighter than usual so the stitches of pearl cotton will lie snug against the fabric. You may find that using a spring needle or darning foot will give your hooped work better control. Before you start the embroidery, take one stitch and bring the bobbin thread to the top of the fabric so it doesn't get caught into later embroidery. Stitch slowly, since the needle will be sewing through layers of pearl cotton.

RUCHING

Ruching is another word for gathering or shirring fabric. It comes from the medieval Latin meaning "bark." You can experiment with hand-basting stitches in simple patterns and pulling the loose strings to ruche or gather. The bubbles that result can be stuffed individually on the underside before pulling them tight. Popular names for this technique are popcorn or bubble stitching (Fig. 7.14, bottom right). To make a large flower center from this textured fabric, use a firm plastic or metal shape as a base. Cover and pad it slightly to form a dome. Jar covers or frozen juice can lids work well for this base.

Judi Cull of Sacramento, California, has perfected the method of ruching with a sewing machine. She uses elastic thread in the bobbin and rayon or metallic thread on top. Wind the bobbin without stretching the elastic thread. Set the bobbin tension slightly looser than normal. This should be good enough to stretch the elastic as you stitch.

To make a ruched flower center, use a 5" (127mm) or 7" (178mm) spring hoop. You can hoop a single layer of fabric or include a piece of fleece underneath the fabric for "stuffed" bubble stitching. Stitch tiny circles from 1/4" (6.4mm) to 1/2" (13mm) in diameter, filling an area twice as large as you will need for the flower center. When you release the fabric from the hoop, you will be delighted to see that each circular shape is filled with the fleece backing and the stitched area has shrunk because of the ruching. For tighter gathers, hold an iron over the wrong side and steam the elastic to encourage further shrinkage. Do not touch the fabric with the iron.

Prepare this texturized fabric by stay-stitching where it will be cut. Because the fabric is too thick to be used in the usual way to cover a button, allow enough fabric to wrap to the wrong side for gathering. Zigzag over a cord near the cut edge for the drawstring.

A large disc covered with ruching can be glued into the center of many types of fabric flowers. For others, you may want to glue a shank button or the back half of a covered button to the back of the ruched flower center. This will allow you to pull the covered flower center snugly in place, with a string or wire attached to the shank. The string or wire will pass through the middle of the flower and down to the stem or secure on the back of the flower.

Wrapped Beads

A wrapped-bead flower center can be made from various shapes with fabric wrapped tightly around them with a single thread on the bottom side. The shapes include beads and cotton balls, as well as an assortment of scented things. The color and quality of the beads don't matter necessarily because the fabric will cover them, unless you use a transparent fabric like tulle or chiffon.

SINGLE BEADS

Starting with beads, consider large round or half-round beads. Craft stores carry a raspberry-shaped bead in several sizes. Whichever bead you choose, you have the option of simply covering it with fabric or adding a single stitch by hand that goes from the bottom of the bead to the top and down through the hole again. After you pull the stitch snug, the fabric will pull down into the bead's hole. Lycra is perfect because it stretches over the beads so easily (Fig. 7.15, top left).

Try this technique using a fabric-covered cotton ball instead of a bead (Fig. 7.15). Take a few more stitches and add a seed bead if you like the texture. Another variation is to bring all stitches through the same center hole, but allow the thread to wrap around the outer edge of the cotton ball. When pulled snug, the thread will divide the shape like the

Fig. 7.15 Clockwise from top left: wrapped pony bead, cotton ball with several stitches, stamen attached to a wooden bead, and cotton ball with one stitch in the center.

outside of a pumpkin (Fig. 7.15). This center is ideal for poppies, especially if you use dark-colored or black thread to wrap the colored shape.

Another idea is to use a single bead to create five stamen and form a calyx at the same time (Fig. 7.15, bottom right). Bring the ends of 25 8"-long (20cm) strands of thread together and roll them together with a drop of white glue. The glue will dry quickly and you can thread the strands through a bead at the same time with this stiffened end, working as if it were the end of a shoelace. Pull the threads until you have about 4" (102mm) on either side of the bead. Tie the two sides in a square knot next to the bead and add a drop of glue to secure the knot.

Separate all the threads and tie groups of five with a large knot at each end, making the stamen. The threads don't have to be all the same length. Cut the ends by the knot and finish by rubbing white glue along the length of each stamen. This will bundle the threads and help them hold a graceful shape.

The single bead at the base of the stamen simulates the calyx, and it can be padded if it isn't large enough for the flower. However, this is a good time to use those large wooden beads that you have been saving from past projects. Before surrounding this flower center with petals, you can wrap the bead with a square of fabric and padding if necessary. The four corners of the fabric gather around the stamen when you wrap and tie a thread just above the bead. Layers of tulle or sheer fabrics make a soft finish for this step.

Now the petals can be stitched or glued around the flower center. Wrap a wire for the stem around the bundle and finish the flower by covering the calyx as described in Chapter 8. If you have used a bead with a large hole and you haven't already filled it with thread for the stamen, pass the stem wire through, too. Twist the end near the base of the bead or place the center of the wire at the bead and twist the two lengths together. This doubled wire will make a stronger stem.

TASSEL CENTERS

The tassel stamen is a dimensional project using free-motion machine embroidery to make a tassel-like center. The beaded strings of straight stitching shoot from the flower center like fireworks (Fig. 7.16). A fuller version of this tassel center appears in the book *Tasselmania*, by Nancy Welch of Woodside, California. It includes my tassel earrings using the same technique used for making tassel flower centers. Tassel earring kits are available from Aardvark Adventures, which provides thread, findings, and beads. My technique is unique because the Welch tassels are usually made by hand and mine use a sewing machine.

Fig. 7.16 Machine-stitched tassel center with seed beads attached with the sewing machine.

I use rayon threads for the tassel stamen because they absorb the dissolved water-soluble stabilizer easily and will hold a shape better than metallic threads. But I like the sparkle of metallic threads. A compromise is to use a rayon thread on top and a fine metallic in the bobbin. Rayon will stitch easily while attaching beads and will hold a shape longer, yet the metallic still highlights the stamen.

Your choice of beads is limited only by the need to have a hole large enough to slide all the way up the machine needle and less than ¼" (6.4mm) in diameter. If the bead is larger, the needle bar will not be able to go all the way down, even though the machine will attempt to force it to do so. The result may be a shattered bead with parts flying everywhere and the machine's timing being thrown off. Neither of these is good news, but both are easy to avoid by checking the size of the beads and the hole in each bead before stitching. This takes only a few minutes.

1 Draw a 3" (76mm) circle with reference marks about every ¼" (6.4mm) on the perimeter, on a piece of water-soluble stabilizer using a permanent pen, such as Pigma Micron or Sharpie (Fig. 7.17). Place a second layer of water-soluble stabilizer under the one with the pattern and put both pieces into a 5" (140mm) spring hoop.

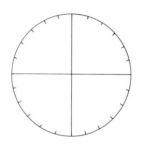

Fig. 7.17 Layout for the tassel center.

2 Put a 5mm jump ring in the center of the pattern, secure with glue stick, and put a 1" (25mm) square of water-soluble stabilizer over it.

3 Before you start the embroidery, make sure the beads you select will slide up a #70 (10) machine needle. You will need a total of 32 beads for this pattern. The beads may all be the same color or you can alternate the color with every other bead.

Machine Setup

Stitch length: 0
Stitch width: 0
Feed dogs: down or covered
Presser foot: none
Upper tension: normal, balanced with bobbin
Lower tension: normal
Needle size: #60 (8)–#70 (10)
Top thread: rayon

Bobbin thread: rayon
Hoop: 5″ (127mm) spring
Stabilizer: water-soluble

4 Do your first line of stitching on one of the four lines dividing the circle. Your control of the work and the resulting stitch quality will be best when the line of stitching goes from the jump ring toward you, back to the jump ring. Then pivot the work to sew the next line.

Take the first stitch just outside the jump ring, then pull the bobbin thread to the top. Turn the handwheel as you stitch over the jump ring. Take the second stitch on the inside of the ring, and then take another stitch on the outside of the ring. Stitch out to the edge of the circle, attach one bead at the tip of the radius, stitch back toward the center, and attach a second bead about ¼″ (6.4mm) from the first one (Fig. 7.18).

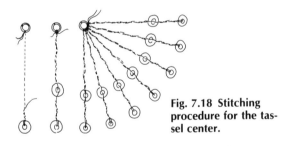

Fig. 7.18 Stitching procedure for the tassel center.

The line of stitching going toward the center is not meant to be exactly on top of the previous one. Instead, it should be on either side of it occasionally over it. Turn the handwheel as you stitch into and out of the jump ring. Be sure to hold the beginning thread tails next to the jump ring as you proceed with the next ten radii. This will secure the thread tails; then you can snip them. If you forget to attach a bead, or you attach a bead of the wrong color, keep going. You will never know the difference once the work is three-dimensional.

If the thread breaks, remove the work from

the machine and trim the threads. Continue stitching by overlapping about five short stitches. Finish by stitching around the outside of the jump ring three times using short stitches.

5 Trim the water-soluble stabilizer ¼″ (6.4mm) from the outside circle. Cut a ½″ (13mm) slit between two rows of stitching. Tie a loop of thread to the jump ring (Fig. 7.19). Soak the piece in warm water for five minutes to remove the stabilizer. Massage the gel out of the threads and soak. Rinse the embroidery until the water-soluble stabilizer is no longer visible and you can't feel it. Then hang the embroidery to dry. This washing procedure will leave the stamen limp, which is suitable for some flowers. If you want the flowers to hold their shape and remain stiff, dissolve scraps of water-soluble stabilizer in the rinse water before soaking the embroidery. For quicker drying, use a hair dryer.

Fig. 7.19 Drying method for the tassel center.

KNOTTED LOOPS OR CORDS

This method of making stamens uses an assortment of threads and cords but doesn't involve any sewing. Fabric stores carry two sizes of a satin cord called "rattail" that comes in many rich colors and is perfect for larger flowers. Tie a single knot, wrapping the cord twice and pulling snug. Tie the two lengths together with construction thread and put a drop of craft glue at the base of the knot to keep it from slipping. To hide the thread ends, thread them through a needle and run them inside the length of the rattail (Fig. 7.20).

Knotted loops can be made using a combination of construction, rayon, or metallic threads (Fig. 7.21). Color is the main concern, and you can change the color easily by adding more strands of the thread whose color you want to intensify. The strands can be joined by a knot at the end of the loop for each stamen or by a single knot in the center of each loop. For a larger knot, wind the strand two to five times, similar to a surgeon's knot. The strands coming from the knot can be either twisted together or simply coated with a craft glue that will dry clear and add stiffness.

Fig. 7.20 Double-wrapped knot using rattail.

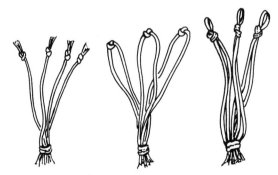

Fig. 7.21 Stamen using multiple strands of thread tied in several ways.

ASSORTED CRAFT STAMENS

The stamens in this section are made by crafting techniques instead of sewing. Threads and beads may be used so these flower centers complement the fabric flowers.

The stalk of the stamen can be made of threads, Mizuhiki (Japanese paper cord), or florist wire (bare or covered). You will want something sturdy for some of the following stamen tips. Acrylic paint can be applied to the tips.

1 If you like the bumpy texture of the berry bead, then many possibilities await you in your kitchen. Grains, peas, beans, cornmeal, seeds, and spices now have a different use! Bend a wire and glue it inside the hole of a wooden bead. Coat the outside of the bead with thick craft glue and roll it in one of the grains or seeds to cover it completely. Keep the natural color or dye or paint the coated beads. Brush on a clear sealer or paint to strengthen the bead cluster (Fig. 7.22A).

2 Colored shapes of bread dough or a polymer clay can be molded on the ends of wire or Mizuhiki stamen.

3 Squeeze a drop of hot or low-temperature glue from a glue gun for the tip of the

Fig. 7.22 (A) Stamen tips with mustard seeds and cornmeal, (B) drop of hot glue, (C) drop of hot glue covered with low-temperature glitter glue, and (D) stamen made of scented beads attached to a wire using low-temperature glue.

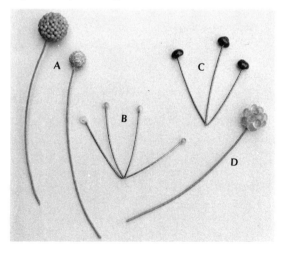

stamen. If you dip the end in water immediately, the hot glue will keep a smooth, round shape (Fig. 7.22B).

4 Glitter Glue Sticks by Crafty Magic Melt make interesting tips on stamen. They work in a low-temperature glue gun that uses these oval-shaped glue sticks. Like hot glue, dip the glittered stamen in water to cool the round shape quickly. For a larger tip, add the glitter glue to a cooled stamen of glue (Fig. 7.22C).

ADDING A SCENT-IMENTAL TOUCH

I have been tempted to tell you how to add scent to the fabric flowers before now, but, to be fair, it is easier to learn the materials and assembly of each fabric flower first. Now we can make substitutions as they are appropriate for the type of scent and a particular flower center.

Potpourri is readily available, and you may even have your own special recipe, but it is difficult to work with for our purposes. Both sachets and potpourris emit a clean, natural scent. Generally, sachet mixtures are chopped, ground, or powdered, while potpourri mixtures are whole or cut. Adding essential oils to the mixtures is optional.

Bath shops sometimes carry fragrance beads that look like clear-colored lentil shapes. They hold their scent for a long time and are easy to use in various ways because of their size. Place a pouch of the beads under the fabric when using a covered button for a flower center. Or bundle a small amount of scented beads in tulle and use it for a flower center all by itself. A cluster of six fragrance beads can be glued to the tip of a single stamen, or a dozen may cover the tip like a tiny pomander (Fig. 7.22D). A low-temperature glue gun works the best, since you will want to mold the beads into the glue with your fingers.

You may also want to try scented paper or sachet. Specialty soaps keep their scent for a long time and can be cut, grated, or shaved to obtain the desired amount. Paper-thin soap leaves can be slipped under the fabric of a covered button. Miniature ¼" (6.4mm) balls of soap could stuff a flower center for a large bloom.

Perhaps you would like your fabric flowers to contain a greater amount of scent for use in a drawer, closet, or dresser top. Attach a small lace sachet pillow or pouch underneath a single flower. Arrange a grouping of small flowers on top of this scented pouch for another attractive idea. A pillow containing potpourri may be constructed from tulle or lace so that you can see the colorful dried ingredients. A pouch containing sachet or grated soap should be made of a fine woven fabric. For larger pillows, place the scented pouch on top of the stuffing before stitching the case closed.

Illuminate the Subject

Battery-operated minilights have found their way into every kind of craft. Now you will find many illuminated novelties, including visors, jewelry, ties, balloons, miniature trees, cake tops, and especially sweatshirts.

MINIATURE LIGHTS AND LEDs

There are two kinds of battery-powered lights (Fig. 7.23). The plastic 5mm LED lights have the larger bulb and are designed for use in apparel, hats, bags, and toys (not for small children) since they have soft 10" (254mm) wires. The LEDs may come in 8, 10, or 15 flashing assemblies of either clear or multicolored lights that will work up to 12 hours. They are lightweight, conveniently powered by four button-cell batteries, and have an on/off switch. The lights are fastened by pushing each one through a hole in the garment and sliding an O-ring over it. The light assembly can be removed easily before washing the garment. A ten-light system was buried in the

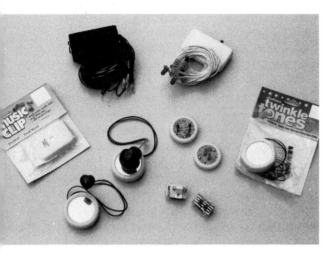

Fig. 7.23 Assorted minilights, LEDs with pin backs, and music buttons.

gravel surrounding the cacti in the dish garden in Chapter 6.

The other kind of battery-powered light is made for use in floral arrangements and craft projects. The glass lights are smaller than the plastic LEDs. The three-volt incandescent lights may be flashing or steady-burn and have wires 6" (152mm) to 36" (914mm) long to accommodate any floral creation, from a boutonniere to a wedding cake. The longer standard 20" (508mm) wires are used for wreaths, balloons, and bouquets. The lights may be clear or multicolored and are usually powered by AA batteries with an on/off switch. Although these lights have been used in garments, they will wear out faster with frequent turning on and off. Also, the glass lights do not fasten to garments as easily as the LEDs.

You might choose to light the center of each fabric flower, or arrange the lights among the flowers. You may also add lights later or move them from one arrangement to another.

Another fun lighting unit, by Darice Inc., is the light button, which can be used to illuminate a cluster of florets or the English loom flowers. You can construct tiny separate petals for your fabric flower or gather a bias strip for a cabbage rose. Attach the petals around each LED with a glue gun. Because you must work in a tight space, use a low-temperature glue gun to prevent burning your fingers. The hotter glue won't harm the electronics and could also be used. The unit is only ½" (13mm) × ⅞" (22mm) with a pin back already attached. The two flashing LEDs may be spaced 7mm or 15mm apart and are powered by two replaceable button batteries.

If you are looking for the complete minilight and sound show for your floral creation, you can use the lights that are attached to a music button. Press the music button to make the lights blink. All the components are small and powered by button cell batteries. In craft stores, you may also find a tiny blinking heart or flashing light buttons for use as jewelry or magnets. The gift of a fabric flower that twinkles and plays music would surely bring a smile to someone special, although such items are not appropriate for small children.

BALLOON LIGHTS

Now for the most unique combination of lights and fabric flowers. "Balloon" flowers are large fabric petals surrounding inflated balloons with a minilight inside each balloon (Fig. 7.24). The petals have a wired edge and veins to hold their shape. Each flower has a plastic rod for the stem, and a small light flashes when the battery pack hidden in the pot is turned on (see Supply Sources). This is a fun display for holidays, parties, or any festive occasion. The arrangement has endless possibilities because the balloons and petals can be changed to suit the event or season. Sequins and jewels can be glued to the inflated balloons using a low-temperature glue gun.

Fig. 7.24 Balloon-light flower with giant fabric petals by Mary Schaudies of Harlingen, Texas.

Fig. 7.25 Fiber optics with beads in the firecracker bouquets on the sleeve caps of "American Pie" jacket by Virgie Fisher of Sacramento, California.

The plastic flower pot can be decorated using some of the techniques explained in Chapter 10 or simply set inside a corded basket or a cachepot that you have made. Weight the base with small rocks or even plastic bags filled with sand. Cover them with Spanish moss, marbles, or soft folds of fabric.

FIBER OPTICS

Fiber optics provide a new method of illumination for the crafter or designer of wearable art. Virgie Fisher has designed numerous garments with a lyrical sense of humor using fiber optics throughout (Fig. 7.25). The hairlike fibers carry the light to each tip and spray out from the flower centers and firecrackers alike. The light will radiate through plastic, glass, or crystal beads secured on the ends of the fibers. The synthetic fibers are sewn into the garment or project and a pocket-size flashlight supplies the power source.

The method of installing fiber optics is simple but fine-tuned from many hours of experimenting. (For fiber-optic kits, see Supply Sources.)

8

Leaves and Stems

Now that your fabric flowers are in bloom, you are ready to complete nature's work by adding leaves and stems. You might be content with the fabric flowers as they are, but adding a touch of greenery will make them even more lifelike. An arrangement of one or more flowers with leaves can make a beautiful presentation. The following information pertains to appliquéd flowers as well as to flowers on stems.

Leaves

Now that you have created your exquisite garden of fabric flowers, it is time to decide on the number and placement of leaves. Before you get caught up in the fun of creating, take a moment to look at the leaf arrangement on plants in your garden or in a nursery or flower shop. Notice that some leaves are single and some are grouped on a single stem. This might be too much greenery. For flowers that are stitched or glued to a background fabric, you may not need much greenery, if any at all, but leaves are a major design factor for fabric flowers on stems.

Leaves help separate and space the flowers, and the green props hold each stem in a natural pose. Like a florist, you can start your arrangement by placing a few branches of leaves, then filling in with flowers.

LEAF PLACEMENT

If you decide to add stems to your flowers, consider first the size and shape of the vase

you will place them in. You may want to make a fabric vase of your own design. If not, will you use a glass vase? Does it have a large opening? Asking these questions may save you time and will help you plan the arrangement so you will not waste leaves that will not be visible.

A vase with a smaller opening holds the flowers upright and makes it easier to arrange them. Adding crinkled foil or marbles to the bottom of any vase will hold the stems in place, too. If you use a vase with a larger opening, plan to attach the lower leaves 1" or 2" (25mm or 51mm) below the top of the vase. Most of the greenery will be visible above the opening and these lower leaves will prop the stems in place.

If you use a glass or transparent vase, fill it with cellophane, sheer fabric, buttons, beads, necklaces, or curled gift-wrap ribbons. Have fun doing the unexpected. Attach a few leaves farther down the stems so they will be visible through the vase. This will break the monotony of bare stems and help hold the arrangement in place.

You can add leaves to fabric flowers on stems at any time. I make lots of leaves and satin stitch them in pairs to a wire so the tips extend ½" (13mm) beyond the ends of the wire (Fig. 8.1). The bases of the leaves are ½" (13mm) apart near the center of the wire. I wrap each set of leaves around a stem until I have covered the coils with the leaves. Add a drop of glue to the coils if you want to attach them permanently.

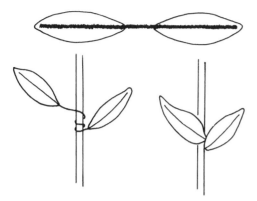

Fig. 8.1 Method of satin stitching wire to a pair of fabric leaves and attaching them to a wire stem. Bend the leaves to cover the coils.

SECURING LEAVES TO AN APPLIQUÉD FLOWER

Whether you secure your blooms to a garment or decorate a pillow, there is nothing more distracting than leaves that are too large for the flower or that are awkwardly placed at strange angles. These are unfortunate mistakes and you can avoid them easily if you keep in mind a few rules. First, each leaf should look as if its stem originates from the center of the flower, the way spokes radiate from the center of a wheel (Fig. 8.2). As you might expect, an odd number of leaves is the rule of thumb. Even though you might make them from the same pattern, leaves will be more natural looking if you extend them in slightly different lengths beyond the flower's edge.

You might decide that the leaves you have carefully sewn are too big for the flower. Unless you are prolific and have tons of time, try to adapt them to your current project and make smaller leaves the next time. Using ingenuity will set your garden apart from your neighbor's! Imagine a few boulders and river rock set among the flowers in a garden—a different and an artistic arrangement, right? So who has to know what lies beneath them?

Fig. 8.2 Shadow appliqué on sweater made from silk flowers and tulle. Flower centers are bartack stars and beads, with detail.

Oversized leaves can still be used if you make a fold or a series of tucks at the center when attaching them. Place the tucks closer to the flower center so a smaller portion of the leaf extends beyond the flower's edge. To reduce the bulk of an oversized leaf, straight-stitch along the lower half where you would like the new smaller leaf to finish. Cut away excess fabric and zigzag or satin-stitch the new edge. This edge may never show, but this clean finish will add a professional touch to your special project.

WIRED EDGES

The technique of stitching wire along the edges of leaves is explained in Chapter 6. A lightweight wire can be used in conjunction with a foot that has a center guide or even with an edge-stitching foot. Lightweight wire is better suited to petals with smooth, simple curves, such as the large petals used with the balloon lights in Chapter 7. The wire also will work on simple leaf patterns. Leaves with undulating edges will be more difficult to edge with wire because you cannot satin-stitch tight curves easily if you use a foot.

THREE WAYS TO ADD WIRE

You will find that a single wire placed down the center of a flat leaf may be all you need to shape it. This is the simplest touch you can add to liven up greenery. The larger, more detailed leaves with lobes will benefit from some additional wires used to form veins that cross the main vein.

Florist wire is easily found at craft stores and is available either plain or covered. My preference is the covered wire because the satin stitching will stay in place better as a result of friction. Covered wire enables you to glue-stick or actually fuse the wire to fabric. The package usually describes it as cloth-covered wire and it may be green or white.

Wire sizes are measured in gauges: the smaller the number, or gauge, the thicker the wire. All the stems on the flowers and ivy in this book use 18-gauge wire, including the looped flowers in Chapter 6, where the wire is inserted into a craft cord covered with fabric. The Leaf Spray in this chapter uses 24 gauge. The three veins in the ivy leaves and edges of giant petals like those in the balloon lights use 20 gauge. The light wire inserted in the $\frac{1}{8}$" (3.2mm) bias tubes forming the petals in the Nosegay of Loops in Chapter 6 is 32 gauge.

To sew the wire on top of a finished leaf, use a 2-$\frac{1}{2}$ width, satin-stitch length and an open-toe appliqué foot. Backstitch at the beginning and the end of the satin stitching. Secure the stitching with a drop of seam sealant. When joining a 24-gauge leaf stem to an 18-gauge main stem, I use the Pearls 'N Piping foot by Creative Feet, which has a deep groove on the underside like a welting, piping, or bulky overlock foot.

The second method of attaching wire to a leaf keeps the wire inconspicuous and is done after edging the leaf or petal shape. This technique is best for petals or leaves made from a single layer of fabric and when you might not want to secure the wire by the obvious use of a satin stitch. Use telephone wire or a 32-gauge cloth-covered wire and enclose it in a pintuck sewn on the wrong side of the finished shape. The fabric should be folded with right sides together with the fine wire in the fold (see Fig. 6.24). Put glue stick on the wire first if you need help holding it in place. Sew a straight stitch from the base of the shape toward the tip. The wired pintuck may go only halfway or extend to the end of the petal or leaf's tip. The wire doesn't need to be as long as the pintuck. Backstich or tie to secure the stitching.

A third way to add wire is to place it between two fabric shapes before fusing them together. Place the wire in the center of the petal or leaf $\frac{1}{2}$" (13mm) from the tip. Let it extend from the base to form a stem. Satin-stitch over the wire using an appliqué foot. Since the two pieces of fabric are fused together, you can use any decorative stitch—not just the satin stitch—as long as you can sew over the wire. The fabric may be trimmed next to the stitching after it is completed.

STITCHING A WIRE VEIN

A wire vein can be satin-stitched on top of the leaves after completing all the other stitching. By using a rayon thread similar to the color of the leaf, the vein will remain inconspicuous, except for the raised stitching over the wire. Some leaves do not need a wire for shaping because they already have enough body for stability and an interesting form. In this case, sew a wire to the base of the leaf to serve as a stem.

An alternative to using wire is to couch Mizuhiki, a Japanese paper cord, on the finished leaf or flower. The cord will make a more decorative vein since it is metallic and the single strands are not as stiff as wire. Directions for its use on edges are contained in Chapter 3 under Machine-Stitched Edges.

Set your sewing machine for a 2-½ width and a satin-stitch length with embroidery thread on top and in the bobbin. Consider using a metallic thread in the bobbin and rayon on top. An open-toe appliqué foot will make sewing over wire quick and easy. A pintucking foot with a groove in the center may be useful when the wires don't overlap or curve too much.

Determine the length of the wire by placing it on top of the leaf. Add a little more for the stem. You can also attach another leaf at the other end of the same wire and twist it onto a stem. Assemble the branches in the same way by adding pairs of leaves to the main stem (see Fig. 8.1). If you intend to twist the leaves onto each other or onto other stems, coil the end of an extra-long stem for a decorative effect, like the delicate tendrils on a grapevine.

Cut the florist wire with wire cutters and straighten the ends of the stem if it bends after cutting. Cut the wire to the desired length just as you are ready to stitch it to the leaf. Place the wire on the leaf ¼" (6.4mm) from the tip of the leaf and use a 2-½ width to anchor and bury the end of the wire with satin stitching. This buildup of stitches at the end of the wire keeps it from poking through the satin stitches later.

Continue to sew down the wire with a zig-zag to hold it in place. Go back over it with a satin stitch. Backstitch at the end of the wire. By changing to a straight stitch and a left or right needle position, you can secure the stitching on one side of the wire. Add a drop of seam sealant or craft glue on the last stitches, then cut the thread tails.

If you want to add more wires on a leaf, work with an even number for convenience. Make a sharp bend in the wire where a pair

of extra veins intersect the main vein. This technique was used for Leaf E of the Machine-Stitched Leaf Spray in this chapter. It was also used for Leaf A and Leaf C, which are sprigs of seven and three leaves. Start at the tip of a horizontal vein and satin-stitch over it toward the bend (Fig. 8.3). Turn the leaf and continue on the other side, finishing at the tip. After you have stitched the horizontal veins, satin-stitch the center one that extends to become the stem.

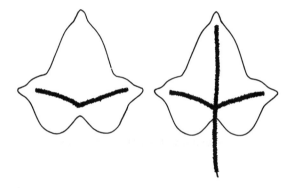

Fig. 8.3 Satin stitching more than one wire to a leaf.

If you have good control with machine embroidery, you might want to do this stitching in free-motion. A darning spring is helpful. This freedom will allow you to stitch in many directions to cover the wires at the intersection. Even though you can maneuver the leaf while stitching, the stitching will be smoother and you will have greater control if you place the leaf on top of a hooped piece of water-soluble stabilizer. The stabilizer will move easily across the bed of the machine and can be torn away later.

The tendrils or coils at the end of each stem are the single wires covered with satin stitching, as in the Machine-Stitched Leaf Spray in the color pages. The top and bobbin threads are not matching but are complementary colors of rayon and metallic threads. You can do this stitching in free-motion, or you can use an appliqué foot. To shape the coils, wrap the finished wire tightly around a ¼" (6.4mm) dowel or pencil and spring open slightly.

ADDING A CALYX

A calyx is the group of small leaves that covers a flower bud. When the flower opens, the calyx cups its underside. You might not need to add this detail to every flower, but it is a nice way to add a finishing touch. In most cases, the calyx provides a convenient way to hide the assembly stitches on the flower base and stem (Fig. 8.4). Some flowers can be dressed up by using large novelty beads for the calyx. Antique gold or silver beads will add a distinctive style to the flowers. Slide a large bead up the wire stem and glue it to the back of the flower. Add a smaller round bead and glue it to the larger one.

Let's make the calyx in the easiest way without sacrificing a professional finish. You may need to cut the base of the petals so they gradually taper to the size of the stem. Thread a hand sewing needle and take a few short stitches in the calyx area. With the needle still threaded, wrap around the flower base three times and pull until the thread is snug. Take a few stitches to secure the wraps. Bundle the base of the petals, then cover it with craft

glue. Carefully wrap a heavy decorative thread to make a calyx over the base of the petals.

You may prefer to use small fabric leaves to cover the calyx area. Make as many as you need, about four or five. Glue them in place and cover the ends with wrapping as you continue to wrap toward the end of the stem. Include some additional sprigs of leaves at various places along the stem while wrapping.

A fabric calyx may be cut from a 3" (76mm) circle using pinking, scalloping, or wavy-edge shears. A flat flower pattern also makes a good calyx. The first method is to run a gathering stitch so that the fabric calyx will cup around the base of the petals (Fig. 8.5A, B). The second method is to push a wire through the center of the calyx, then wrap a thread around the wrong side of the calyx (see Figure 8.5C). Then pull the calyx up to cup the base of the calyx; gather to finish (Fig. 8.5D).

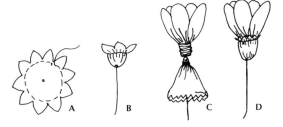

Fig. 8.5 Attaching a fabric calyx with hand-stitching.

Candle cups are a popular wooden shape, while bean-pot cups and tulip candle cups are less well known but make a suitable calyx. Small and medium cups were used in Chapter 6 for the calyxes in the Nosegay of Loops. Craft stores usually carry a small assortment of these wooden items, but a woodworking store will have a selection to satisfy your every whim. A wooden calyx can top a wooden dowel or a heavy-gauge wire stem. The bases of tightly wrapped petals can be glued into the cups.

Fig. 8.4 Five ways to make a calyx (left to right): (1) Cover the base of the petals with fabric, (2) use large beads or (3) jewelry findings that cover the base, (4) wrap the base with heavy threads, and (5) glue the base inside wooden candle cups.

Circle Leaf

Circle leaves are suitable for almost every kind of fabric flower. For compatibility, use the same kind of fabric for the leaf that you used for the flower. Also experiment by using the wrong side of the original flower fabric, especially on fabrics such as iridescent satins. Or use two layers of fabric for the leaves if you have used sheers for the flower. Experiment by selecting a different color for the inner layer.

The circle leaf is fast to make because you don't have to turn corners. It is suitable for woven fabrics and is especially successful in sheers. Circle leaves were used for the gingham leaves on the straw hat in the color section. These leaves do not have stems. Fold a circle of fabric in half with right sides together and the bias on the fold. Stitch along the edge to make a fat little leaf that rolls back on itself (Fig. 8.6, left). For a long, slender leaf, stitch as shown in Figure 8.6, right, then cut away half of the width. Use a gathering foot and a machine set up for gathering—a long stitch length and very tight top tension. The stitching will serve two purposes: to gather and to make ¼″ (6.4mm) seams at the same time (Fig. 8.7). Leave a ¾″ (19mm) opening on one end for turning inside out. Use hemostats to turn the leaves. Pull the seam open and shape the leaf with the same offset.

Basic Flat Leaf

Make the basic flat leaf by fusing two pieces of fabric with wrong sides together. Cut the leaf shapes from the fabric; then satin-stitch a wire stem down the center (Fig. 8.8). Place a 24-gauge wire in the center of the leaf, ½″ (13mm) down from the tip of the leaf. Satin-stitch, using a 2-½″ width and an appliqué foot. Near the base of the leaf, change to a 4 width so the stitching will wrap the base of the leaf around the wire. Sew over the wire for ½″ (13mm) and place the base of another leaf under the wire. Continue satin-stitching the wire to the second leaf (see Fig. 8.8). Cut the wire so it will finish ½″ (13mm) from the tip of the second leaf. Stitching on the cut edge isn't necessary since the fabric is fused. The simplicity of this leaf makes it a good one for adding color with fabric paint or paint sticks. Any leaf shape can be made this way.

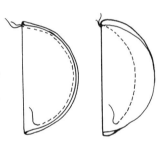

Fig. 8.6 Circle leaf construction without adding wire stems. The leaf is made from a circle folded in half. On the left, a short, full leaf. On the right, a long, slender leaf made by stitching a wider seam.

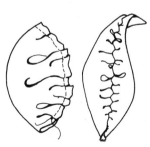

Fig. 8.7 With the right sides of the circle leaf together, sew a gathering stitch on the seam line and leave an opening at the bottom for turning. The turned leaf (right) rolls back on itself.

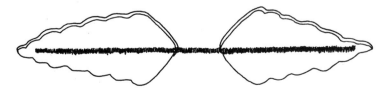

Fig. 8.8 The basic flat leaf is cut from two layers of fabric fused with wrong sides together. A wire stem is satin stitched to a pair of leaves.

Gathered Leaves

Gathered leaves were made for the Christmas arrangement (Fig. 6.5). The fun part of using sheer fabrics with this method is that the seam line isn't obvious, so it is hard to figure out how the leaves were made. The construction is similar to the circle leaves, except that you can use any almond-shape pattern with the center vein line on the fold of the fabric (Fig. 8.9). Satin-stitch a wire stem on top of the seam. The leaves are designed so you can wrap a pair of leaves around a stem until you have covered the leaf wire between them. These leaves offer infinite possibilities since they can be moved to different flowers or all be wrapped on the same stem to make a sprig of leaves. If you want to secure them permanently, add a drop of glue on the coil before you cover with the leaves.

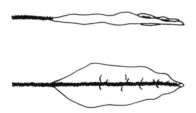

Fig. 8.9 The gathered leaves are turned with the right sides out, and the seam is rolled to the center. The stem (wire) is sewn on top of the seam with a satin stitch.

To economize on fabric, start at one corner and fold on the bias with right sides together for one leaf. Pin in the center of the leaf before you cut it out and remove the pin after sewing. Refold the bias and cut out more leaves. You will find that after you cut a few you won't even need a pattern.

Set the sewing machine for a gathering stitch as done with the circle leaf and make a ¼″ (6.4mm) seam, leaving a ¾″ (19mm) opening at the bottom for turning and lock-stitching the beginning and ending of the seam. If you aren't getting enough gathers, apply a slight pressure behind the presser foot to keep the fabric from flowing smoothly off the back. The fabric will bunch up and force more gathers. When using sheer fabrics, sew all the leaves and trim to ⅛″ (3.2mm) allowance.

Turn all the leaves inside out. Roll the seam open until it is near the center. Attach a wire stem to pairs of leaves as you would do for the basic flat leaves. This time the wire will be placed on top of the gathered seam and the opening at the base of the petal will be closed up with the wide stitch.

Padded Leaves

A quick method for padding leaves is to make a gathered leaf as previously instructed, then insert a piece of stuffing with hemostats. Finish by attaching a wire stem the same way it was done for the gathered leaves (Fig. 8.10). You will be pleased to see how fast you can make these leaves. This technique is perfect for almond leaf shapes of all sizes. Texture can be stitched onto the fabric before it is sewn into a leaf.

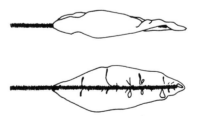

Fig. 8.10 The padded leaves are constructed exactly like the gathered leaves, but a little stuffing is inserted before the wire is attached.

PROJECT: ENGLISH IVY

I have always admired the texture created from stitching wrinkled fabric. This project uses techniques you would normally avoid for flawless, unpuckered embroidery. The patterns may be drawn in any direction on the fabric and placed loosely in the hoop, and, finally, the leaves are steamed to bring out more wrinkles. Create English ivy from soft, supple suede cloth (Fig. 8.11), which comes in rich winter colors. Unlike Ultrasuede, this light-weight knit puckers and curls naturally into leaf shapes. By selecting thread a shade lighter than the fabric, your stitching will be inconspicuous and the texture will predominate.

It is tempting to make ivy in an unusual designer color to coordinate with a room's decor, rather than using just another green. How about off-white ivy with gold, silver, or copper veins for an off-white bathroom? Follow these instructions and learn the tricks that will make this project a success. All the steps are done in assembly-line fashion so they are completed efficiently. A standard 18-gauge, 18″ (457mm) florist wire will accommodate ten leaves. Enlarge the desired ivy pattern so you will have three or four sizes of leaves (Fig. 8.12). Other ivy patterns are provided in Chapter 11 and can be made using the same method as for English ivy.

Fig. 8.12 These patterns for English Ivy should be enlarged to double this size.

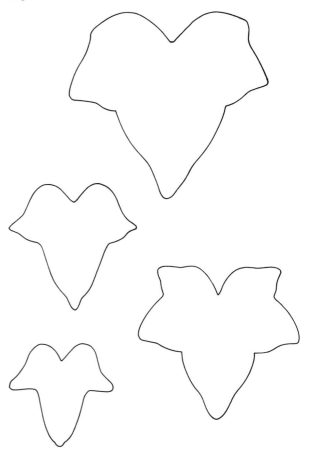

Fig. 8.11 English Ivy made from a single layer of suede cloth. Wires are fused under each leaf and each branch is assembled with satin stitching.

Supplies

1 yd. of suede cloth, 24- and 18-gauge cloth-covered florist wire, fusible web, rotary cutter/pad, glue stick, Teflon sheet, press cloth, wire cutters, soldering iron, rayon in shade lighter than fabric, tan for stems in rayon, two extra bobbins, piping foot.

1 Make a template for each leaf. Draw the outline of several leaves ½″ (13mm) apart on the right side of the fabric. The Pigma Micron pen gives a fine line. A half-yard of this 60″-wide (1.5m) fabric will make more than 100 leaves in assorted sizes.

2 Use a sliver of soap or disappearing pen to mark the five veins on each leaf.

3 Use matching rayon thread on top and bottom and set your sewing machine for balanced tension. Use a 5″ (127mm) spring hoop and place it on the first leaf. (You will move the hoop for each leaf.) Hold the hoop partially compressed with one hand and, with your other hand, pull the fabric toward the center of the hoop. This is how I loosen this fabric in the hoop so the stitching will pucker it slightly but not enough to stitch tucks.

4 Do the stitching with a free-motion setup (Fig. 8.13). Make the veins near the base of the leaf first, followed by the next pair and then the main center vein. Move the hoop as if you are sketching the veins, or in the same way you would make a feather stitch. Lock the stitching with tiny stitches and trim the thread. Don't lose sleep over making the leaves perfect. This is a free-spirited, artistic project. Details will not be noticeable, and now is the time to enjoy the stitching process rather than getting fussy about missing the line.

5 When you have finished all the veins, cut out the leaves with scissors or a soldering iron. Remember, suede cloth is a knit and will not ravel. Again, don't worry about perfection. Cut out the leaves and enjoy their imperfections—just as they appear in nature. The sol-

Fig. 8.13 Stitch five veins on each leaf using a free-motion embroidery setup with rayon thread in a light shade of the leaf color.

dering iron gives a fine darkened edge to the leaves. Remember to hoop the fabric to hold it in tension for sizzling the edges with a soldering iron.

6 Each leaf has two wires that finish ¼″ (6.4mm) from the edge of the leaf—one for the center vein and one for the vein on each side of it. Cut 24-gauge wire into suitable lengths for all the leaves. The wire for the center vein should be 2″ (51mm) longer than the leaf. The other wire will be bent in the middle where it intersects the center wire.

7 Use a rotary cutter to cut ⅛″ (3.2mm) strips of light- or medium-weight fusible web (without the paper backing). You will need about 6″ for each leaf or approximately 15 yards so you can fuse the cloth-covered wire to the back of the leaves. This process works efficiently if you cut the fusible web to the necessary lengths and use a dot of glue stick to hold it in place while fusing. Otherwise static electricity will make them jump.

8 Place three leaves at a time on the ironing board with the wrong sides facing up. Put the bent wire in place, then put the center wire on top. Cover with a Teflon pressing sheet and press until the fusible web melts and sticks to the Teflon. Carefully turn the sheet over, keeping the leaves stuck to the Teflon, and cover them with a soaking-wet pressing cloth (a bandanna is perfect). Press again. This shot of steam causes the web to shrink back around the wire and penetrate the fabric. Remove the leaves after the Teflon has cooled. This very strong bond is barely visible if the fusible web has been cut narrow.

9 Use a light tan or green embroidery thread to satin stitch the stems with an appliqué foot. Start the stitching at the base of the leaf, attaching the last ¼″ (6.4mm) of the leaf to the center wire using a 2-½ width. Continue down the wire and stop ¼″ (6.2mm) from the end. Finish all the leaves this way.

10 Assemble the branches, starting at the tip, and use no more than ten leaves in graduated sizes. The number of leaves per size isn't critical because all the branches should be different. Make the leaf bud at the tip of the branch from a scrap of suede cloth about the size of a nickel. Attach it to the end of an 18-gauge wire with thread wrapping (Fig. 8.14). You must use a foot with a deep groove when assembling the branches. The Pearls 'N Piping foot or a cording foot will accommodate satin stitching over two wires.

Normally you would position yourself with the needle directly in front of you. To assemble the branches, move your chair to the left of the machine so that the branch wire feeds straight into the machine without bending.

Start the 4-width satin stitch at the base of the leaf bud, covering the thread wrapping. Continue sewing over the wire for about 2″ (5cm). Lift the presser foot and insert the first small leaf from the back. The tip of the leaf should be even with the leaf bud and its stem

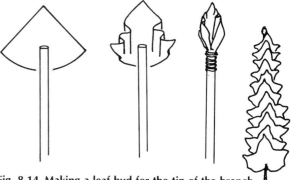

Fig. 8.14 Making a leaf bud for the tip of the branch.

Fig. 8.15 To assemble a branch, start with the smallest leaves and finish with an orderly stack.

should be on top or next to the large wire. Satin-stitch over both wires. Usually the last ¾″ (19mm) of the stems is attached to the main wire. Sew the first ⅜″ (10mm) over the main wire, then add the next leaf. Repeat until the branch is done, continuing the satin stitch to the end of the wire (Fig. 8.15). Use a seam sealant on the last stitches.

11 Shape the leaves by bending every other leaf to alternate sides. Arch the stems slightly so they aren't too stiff. Push the sides of the leaf toward the center to add individual character to each one. After selecting a vase for the ivy, curve the main branch to suit the display. If the stem is too long, just bend it to shorten.

PROJECT: MACHINE-STITCHED LEAF SPRAY

I have always loved the bold colors of fall, and the weathered leaves of lacelike texture capture my interest as well (Fig. 8.16). The following techniques for creating five different leaves are a combination of ideas gleaned from Philip Pepper and a few variations he inspired. Like me, he has found new ways to

have fun with the sewing machine and water-soluble stabilizer.

These leaf patterns will work up beautifully in threads using fall colors. However, don't limit yourself to this color range. The same leaves would be classic in subdued heirloom or Victorian tones. By adding a little more

Fig. 8.16 Leaf spray using a designer set of ten colors of Natesh rayon thread from Aardvark Adventures.

Fig. 8.17 Pattern for the machine-stitched leaves should be enlarged to twice this size.

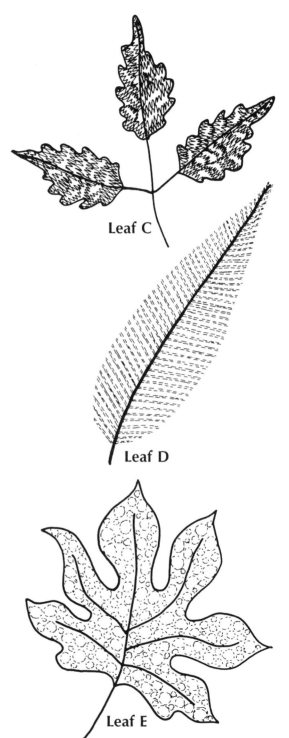

Leaf C

Leaf D

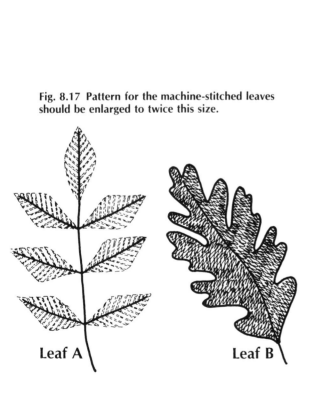

Leaf A

Leaf B

Leaf E

color, you can warm up to country or Southwest hues. And why not get wild with color and end up with a bold, ethnic, or comic mood?

The following directions are for the five styles of leaves. Specific differences are described later for each leaf. The general order is (1) stitch, (2) add wire veins, (3) trim excess stabilizer, (4) rinse off stabilizer, (5) shape and (6) dry.

1 Enlarge the leaf patterns in Fig. 8.17 to the size you wish, then draw on water-soluble stabilizer with ½" (13mm) spacing between leaves. When you add wire stems later, you can position the hoop anywhere over the wires.

2 Use a 5" (127mm) or 7" (178mm) spring hoop to hold the stabilizer with the pattern on it, plus another piece underneath. Position the hoop around a single leaf and follow the appropriate directions below for stitching. Set your machine for free-motion embroidery.

Machine Setup

Feed dogs: down or covered
Presser foot: none
Upper tension: normal or balanced to bobbin
Lower tension: normal
Needle size: #70 (10) to #90 (14)
Top thread: rayon or metallic
Bobbin thread: rayon or metallic
Hoop: 5" (125mm) to 7" (178mm) spring
Stabilizer: water soluble

Supplies

assorted rayon and metallic threads for leaves, extra bobbins, 12" × 12" nylon organdy for leaves, soldering iron, 24-gauge cloth-covered wire

3 After you have completed the embroidery for each leaf, you are ready to attach the wire vein and stem. See the beginning of this chapter for instructions on adding wire to the leaves. Use 24-gauge wire for this project.

4 Before washing away the water-soluble stabilizer, trim the excess to ¼" (6.4mm) from stitching. Soak each leaf individually in a bowl of warm water. Wash and shape one leaf at a time. Massage the leaf under water until the gel from the stabilizer dissolves. Some will remain in the threads and act as a starch when drying. Pat dry with a terry-cloth towel to remove excess moisture.

Use a hair dryer to blow the threads apart and give fullness to the leaf's shape. Turn the leaf and dry from the other side for more shaping. It will take only a minute before the leaves assume character. Allow the leaf to air-dry once you have achieved the desired natural shape. When the leaf is completely dry, shape the wires and assemble the leaves by twisting the stems together. The remaining ends can be coiled to make tendrils.

STITCHING DIRECTIONS FOR LEAVES

Leaf A. Draw each leaf outline and center vein for this group of leaves on water-soluble stabilizer. I prefer to complete the stitching for each leaf before continuing to the next one. Since there are seven leaves on this sprig, you will connect them later when adding the wire stems.

Use a variegated rayon thread on top and a metallic thread in the bobbin. Set a 0 length/0 width and outline each leaf and the center vein twice with a straight stitch. Stitch parallel rows of straight stitching very close together following the natural grain of the leaf. Be sure to anchor each row of stitching to both the vein and the outline. If you miss, the stitching will not be attached when you wash away the stabilizer later.

Leaf B. This is a heavy, sturdy leaf because of the amount of solid stitching done with a satin stitch and two threads through the needle. Its texture adds variation to the otherwise fragile leaves of thread. Put a piece of tulle on top of the water-soluble stabilizer. Use two rayon threads on top, one solid and one varie-gated, and a #80 (12) needle. One of the rayon colors will be in the bobbin.

Straight-stitch around the leaf and down the center vein twice. Trim the tulle next to the stitching outlining the leaf. Set the machine for a 0 length/3–4 width and satin-stitch par-allel rows, overlapping them slightly. This will create the fabric of the leaf, preferably without any gaps between rows.

Leaf C. This leaf is the lacy, weathered ver-sion of Leaf B. I use a pattern with three leaves on a sprig and an overlay of two differ-ent variegated threads. The pattern creates sparse, haphazard stitching, even though the technique of stitching parallel rows of zigzag is similar to Leaf B.

Straight-stitch around the leaf and down the center twice. Set the machine for a 0 length/4 width. Stitch parallel rows of zigzag (not satin stitch!) and occasionally overlap the rows. I stitch portions of each leaf with a green varie-gated rayon, then change to a light brown variegated rayon to finish each leaf. By over-lapping the second color and not overwhelm-ing the leaf with stitching, you will be creating the illusion of the leaf changing colors.

Leaf D. This leaf is fernlike and graceful in its long, slender shape. The threads give a feathery texture when stitched on water-solu-ble stabilizer and shaped after washing. The stitching procedure is similar to Leaf A, except you will not stitch around the outside edge of the leaf, and you will use only a single-thread in the needle. The rows of straight stitching will not be anchored to this edge.

Draw lines on the leaf pattern every inch to remind you of the stitching direction. It is easy to lose track when the stitching is so dense. You can correct the angle of the rows as you stitch. Straight-stitch the vein two times. Stitch parallel rows of straight stitching very close together, trying not to overlap the rows. This leaf is a good exercise in precision embroi-dery. You may find that it is easier to move the hoop left to right rather than forward and back when stitching the parallel rows.

Leaf E. This leaf is made of embroidered sheer synthetic fabric. My preference is nylon or sparkle organdy. Hoop a single layer of the sheer fabric with the leaf pattern drawn on it. You will not use water-soluble stabilizer for this leaf until you attach the wire stems.

Using rayon thread, outline the leaf three times with straight stitching and fill it entirely with ⅛" to ⅜" (3.2mm to 10mm) circles. Go around each circle three times. Change thread colors and highlight some areas with metallic thread. After attaching the wire, use a fine-tipped soldering iron (or stencil-cutting tool) to burn out some of the circles. Cut out the leaf using the soldering iron instead of scis-sors. See Chapter 3 for tips on using this tool for sizzling edges.

Flower Stems

Flower stems may be made of wire or a nar-row wooden dowel. Your choice depends on the size of the flower and the support it will require for its height. Each kind of stem is covered in a different way. Wire stems can be satin-stitched using a deeply grooved cording foot or a Pearls 'N Piping foot. No matter which type of stem or finishing method you choose, consider attaching the flower center to the stem before adding the petals.

You can finish wire flower stems as you would finish the wire stems on the leaves, by sewing over them with a satin stitch. Secure the threads and remove from the sewing ma-chine. If the flower center is a covered button, the wire can be attached easily. Some flower assemblies allow you to wrap the wire around the center. The fabric flowers that don't offer easy solutions may be glued to a flat spiral of the wire. Add a calyx to any of the flowers as a decorative finish.

Stems of all diameters can be covered with fabric or with a variety of threads, yarns, or ribbons. The technique of wrapping (old as the mummies!) is used in macramé, needle weaving, and in making the bullion stitch for Brazilian embroidery. There are numerous other applications as well, but these three demonstrate the versatility of wrapping.

For our purposes, the fabric strips will be easier to work with if they are less than 1″ (25mm) wide and cut on the bias. Only one edge needs to be folded under since the other will be covered by wrapping. Nonraveling fabric doesn't need an edged turned under or a bias cut. Faux suede, leather, and Lycra work well and provide a rich finish. You can secure the end of the stem by knotting the end of the fabric strip around the stem. Florists often finish the stems on a corsage in this manner when wrapping with ribbon. You also have the option of tucking the end to the inside and gluing or hand-stitching while holding it in place with pins.

WIRE OR METAL ROD STEMS

A heavy 16-gauge cloth-covered florist wire is appropriate for most fabric flowers because of the weight of the petals. Metal rods found in hardware stores come in larger gauges and typically in 36″ (914mm) lengths. They are mild steel and can be bent with pliers and cut with heavy-duty wire cutters.

You might find the need for a pad connected to the metal rod for a support at the base of the flower. First, bend one end of the rod to form a loop, then make a sharp 90-

degree bend so the loop will be perpendicular to the stem (Fig. 8.18A). You can epoxy a button or solder a piece of copper (the size of a small coin) to the loop for the pad. In both cases, you need to learn how to make a strong joint. It is critical that the two materials to be joined are touching as much as possible, surrounded with the epoxy or solder. A large quantity of bonding material between the two surfaces may result in a cold joint that is very weak. Stained-glass artists as well as plumbers and welders can appreciate the skill of this task.

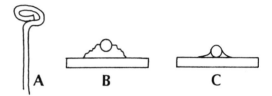

Fig. 8.18 (A) Bend a wire loop for attaching a pad. Side views of a bad (B) and a good (C) joint of epoxy.

WOODEN DOWEL STEMS

Like the metal rod, a wooden dowel will offer more support for a larger flower. Craft or woodworking stores offer an assortment of wooden shapes used for toy making. Wooden-cup shapes may serve both as a support and a calyx. This wooden calyx and stem may be painted. All the flowers made for the Nosegay of Loops in Chapter 6 use a wooden cup for a calyx. See Figure 6.12 for the assembly.

9

How to Display and Wear Fabric Flowers

You probably have a special hat, outfit, or even a vase in mind as you begin your first fabric flowers. By using a matching or a specially selected fabric, you will greatly enhance the presentation and value of the item. Now you will learn ways to mount the flowers with the appropriate hardware or findings for each job. Once you have decided how you want to wear or use your fabric flowers, don't forget to consider adding a scent or miniature lights as discussed in Chapter 7.

Mounting on Jewelry Findings

Thanks to a boon in the retail craft market, jewelry findings are available in fabric stores, as well as in many varieties in local craft stores. Findings have been used in manufacturing for many years, and now we can use them for our own creations (Fig. 9.1).

In addition to wearing a flower as a pin, you can also mount a flower on a button cover, a ⅝" (16mm) brass piece that slides over a standard shirt button, providing a clever way to wear a fabric flower without pinning it to the garment. If you would like to attach a tie tack, bar pin, or stickpin to the back of the flower, use a thick craft glue. Most hot glues will work but aren't necessary for floral decorations or other nonstress projects. Epoxy isn't flexible, but you may need

to use it for gluing metal to metal when you want to add a larger pad to a pin.

Keep a lookout for old jewelry at yard sales. Tie tacks can be reused without any special preparation, while brooches or earrings can be taken apart to give you a flat surface for mounting. You can wear a single flower or several flowers on a sweater at a time. This is why I make each flower with its own pin back instead of permanently grouping flowers in a corsage.

Before mounting the flower, make sure the point of the pin or tie tack is sharp and won't damage the garment. If in doubt, just pin the flower to silk or fine synthetic garments with a straight pin. Cut off an eraser from the end of a pencil and push it on the pin to secure and to prevent sharp pokes.

Some pins may need a larger pad for fastening the flower to the finding properly and

Fig. 9.1 Assortment of jewelry findings for mounting fabric flowers include earrings, pin fasteners, loops, scarf pins, and buckles.

to allow the flower to lie flat when pinned in place. Otherwise the flower will flop forward. Occasionally I add a piece of felt on the inside of the garment to hold the pin in place. An ornamental grill used in jewelry making serves as a decorative pad and a good way to prepare a stickpin.

Clip-on earrings have advantages because the pads come in different sizes. If you prefer hand-stitching to gluing, use a clip-on earring that has several holes in the pad. The pad was designed for stringing beads on a wire and weaving them into the pad. This type of finding is found in older jewelry since bead-cluster earrings were once so popular.

Post earrings have pads in two sizes. For a simple fabric flower like the faux Suede Minis described in Chapter 7, use an earring stud with a pearl or rhinestone for the earring center as well as the fastener. This way, the flowers become interchangeable simply by removing the earring stud.

Thin hoop earrings also become interchangeable when you slide on one or several little flowers. Stitch a bartack with a sewing machine or stitch a small button loop on the back of each flower. The loop should fit snugly around the earring.

Teardrop loops make interesting backings for flowers because of their graceful design. Glue the tiny flowers directly to the bottom of the loop, either centered or to one side. Since teardrop loops usually fasten to a post or an ear wire, you can just as easily attach a jump ring and also wear the flower as a pendant.

Other jewelry ideas include using scarf pins and shoe clips. These accessory items add flair and versatility to the shoes or scarves they adorn. They also can be used to fasten fabric flowers to pockets, lapels, and hat bands.

Don't forget the many possibilities of using a buckle to mount and display the flowers. For temporary use, wrap the wire stems around the buckle. For a permanent decora-tion, attach flowers without stems directly to the buckle with thick craft glue. Smaller buckles work nicely on hatbands as well as on belts. Buckles that fasten without pushing a bar into a hole in the belt are sometimes adjustable and allow you to change the belts by fastening to the buckle with Velcro. The stitching that holds the Velcro in place can be covered with larger flowers.

Hair Ornaments

The popularity of headbands and barrettes provides many ways to wear fabric flowers with different hairstyles. Young girls are not the only ones who can have this fun. Headbands and barrettes are in vogue for all ages. The whimsy or the sophistication is determined by the fabric and size of the flowers used.

Beauty-supply and drug stores sell a variety of barrettes, clips, and bands, and a surprising assortment of metal barrettes and headbands can be found in fabric and craft stores (Fig. 9.2). Plain clip barrettes come in five sizes from 1-½" (13mm) to 3" (76mm) long. Curved oval and rectangular plastic blanks are 4-½" (114mm) long and can be glued on top of any size metal barrette. Use either hot glue or craft glue to secure the flowers and leaves to the blanks. Loops or lengths of narrow ribbons

Fig. 9.2 Hair accessories for mounting fabric flowers include barrettes, clips, combs, and headbands.

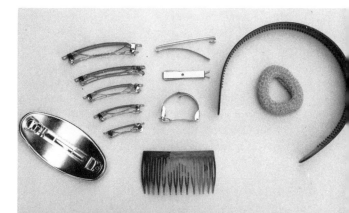

can be added, too. Try using flexible plastic to make a gluing surface for a barrette. The lid from a margarine tub can be cut to any shape.

A different style of barrette comes in oval and rectangular shapes and can be covered with fabric in the same way that you would cover a button. You can either stitch flowers to the fabric, then cover the barrette, or first cover the barrette with fabric and then glue dimensional flowers in place. These barrettes are large and provide a broad surface for mounting flowers.

Crochet a headband or ponytail band using colored or metallic elastic thread. These bands are comfortable and another fun way to wear fabric flowers with quick, easy hairstyles. An elastic headband might even work as a hatband.

Other hair fasteners include elastic bands, plastic banana clips, Clippees, and hair combs. All of these fasten securely to most hairstyles and can be decorated easily with flowers.

Hats

You may have already guessed that fabric flowers can be glued directly onto hats. However, there are so many ways to pin or clip flowers onto hats that I would hesitate mounting the flowers permanently. Instead, attach them individually, mounting each flower on a tie tack, stickpin, tie clip, shoe clip, or clip-on earring back. With a little imagination, you can even clip a decorated barrette to the hat. If you make a hatband from a strip of faux suede, cut small slits for a shoe clip, clip-on earring, or barrette to allow them to grip in the middle of the band.

Baskets and Boxes

Fabric flowers make beautiful additions to baskets and boxes used to store or display other treasures. Wrap and coil flowers on wire

stems onto the handle of a basket. You can either glue or use an extra-long needle to stitch the flowers onto the side of a basket. Depending on the thickness of the basket and how it was woven, you may be able to attach flowers by gluing jewelry findings on their backs. Tie tacks and stickpins may work as well.

Bentwood boxes made in Georgia have an antique flavor and include such styles as cheese boxes, granny buckets, cannisters, bonnet boxes, and placement boxes. Their simplicity makes them perfect for decorating. With their ⅛″ thick sides and ⅜″ lids, they make sturdy keepsakes. See Supply Sources. Inexpensive chipwood boxes are made overseas with very thin sheets of wood and are found at craft stores.

SOFT BOXES

Fabric-covered boxes provide a good surface area for gluing fabric flowers. If the top of the box is padded, use it like a pin cushion for a flower that has a stickpin mounted on back. If you cover the box yourself, consider padding the underside of the cover as well. You will have another place to mount a stickpin.

If you have ever made soft boxes, you can appreciate being able to wash them. Some soft boxes are made from a double thickness of plastic canvas for the stiffener instead of cardboard, then covered with thin batting. Fabric-covered boxes don't always need covers if they are to display or organize often-used items. Make the box in any shape simply by cutting the stiffener for the bottom in a particular shape. Cut the same shape from fleece for both sides of the stiffener. Cut the fabric for the bottom ¼″ (6.4mm) larger on all sides than the bottom stiffener shape.

The number of side pieces depends on the number of angles in the bottom shape. Fabric for the sides may be cut as a single strip. It will measure twice the desired height by the bottom perimeter. Add ½″ (13mm) to each of these measurements to accommodate ¼″

(6.4mm) seams. Inserting the stiffener into the fabric tube will go smoothly if you glue the fleece to the plastic or cardboard stiffener. Wrap a strip of plastic around the padded stiffener to help it slide into place; then pull it away to use on the next side's stiffener. After inserting each fleece-covered stiffener, straight-stitch across the side strip to hold it in place; then insert the next stiffener.

After sewing, stitching, and stuffing the bottom and sides, join them by hand-stitching or gluing. Attach braids or lace with glue for added decoration and finishing.

Corsages

If you have already assembled some fabric flowers with wire stems, they can be arranged quickly and finished in a traditional florist's method by wrapping the wires with tape or ribbon. Be sure to attach the fastener to the wire stems before wrapping so only the necessary hardware will be exposed. Decorative cords or faux suede strips are also good wrapping materials. If you don't have exactly the right color or thickness of cord, combine several kinds of threads or yarns. This will give you unusual results and will probably wrap faster as well.

Even though a corsage is traditionally worn on the upper bodice area of a garment, don't hesitate to pin it on a belt, hat, or purse. If you would like to wear it as a wrist corsage, crochet a band using gold or silver elastic cord. This elastic band is elegant and can be used with different corsages. A cluster of assorted flowers can be pinned separately and changed to accessorize an outfit.

How to Display Flowers When You Aren't Wearing Them

Your lovely blooms deserve to be on display and not stashed away in a box. Whether you have individual flowers or an assembled arrangement like a corsage, let them brighten up any room in the house. Some of these display ideas will allow you to fasten the flowers using the jewelry finding or hardware already attached to the flower.

A grouping of decorator pillows on a bed provides a great surface for attaching fabric flowers with pin backs (Fig. 9.3). Additional flowers can be added to a wreath or garland arrangement in the same room or simply placed in a glass dish on a dresser or shelf. If you have a favorite small vase, set a corsage on top.

In the living room and dining room, fabric flowers and leaves can be placed in the center of a doily or table runner. Flowers on wire stems can be twisted onto an inexpensive wooden embroidery hoop for the base. Paint it or wrap it with fabric before attaching the flowers. As you add more flowers, the hoop will be covered. They can be arranged either to fill the center area or to leave space for a statue or decorator item. This arrangement is also ready for hanging. Flowers that have been assembled as a corsage make a delightful addition to the stem of a candlestick.

There are some clever ways to mount fabric flowers so the display will hang on the wall. Basically, the flowers pin onto a fabric that has been stretched in a hoop or picture frame. When using a hoop, gather the raw edges of

Fig. 9.3 Decorator pillows provide an elegant background for displaying blooming creations.

the fabric to the backside by zigzagging over a heavy cord, as explained in Chapter 2. Glue rows of ruffled lace or fabric around the hoop to finish. You can add more flowers as you make them to match an outfit or occasion.

A large straw hat makes a great background for mounting fabric flowers. You might use a hat that you never intend to wear. A hat richly decorated with flowers makes a wonderful decoration almost anywhere in the house.

10

Sew a Proper Vase

Now that you have created a garden of fabric flowers, it is time to place them in a proper vase. Of course, your china or crystal vase will do in the meantime. A "proper" vase is one created in the same way as your flowers. How else, but with your sewing machine? A fabric mâché vase, padded cachepot, or stiffened sack will display your flowers to perfect effect. The vases are made in a light-hearted spirit of creativity and with the idea that you can do almost anything on a sewing machine. See the color pages for vase ideas.

Fabric-Covered Containers

Fabric-covered vases will add the charm to your special flowers that a ceramic container couldn't begin to offer. You can use just about any kind of container for the fabric mâché vase and padded cachepot since they will be completely covered with fabric. Plaster, gravel, or marbles will add sufficient weight to the bottom.

SELECTING A CONTAINER

A covered vase can be made from a margarine container, frozen juice can, shampoo bottle, glass jar, and even an empty paper towel tube. Don't worry about the stability of the container; just consider its size and shape (Fig. 10.1). Consider using real vases. If you aren't particularly interested in their outer ap-

pearance, then you have a good candidate for covering. Secondhand stores should keep you busy with vases for a while.

Plastic bottles should be trimmed at the top when the opening is too small or you want to remove the threaded section. Submerge the plastic in hot water until it is pliable; then cut it with a knife. A larger base can be glued to the bottom. Combine sections of different containers to get the desired shape, then secure the sections with duct tape or hot glue. A plastic vase composed of a few parts will be sturdy once it is completely assembled and covered.

Fig. 10.1 Silhouettes of a variety of vases to consider when making your own.

PROJECT: FABRIC MÂCHÉ VASE

This technique doesn't include the use of a sewing machine, but it does use fabric. Small prints make a conservative, classic vase, while metallic brocades and prints offer elegance and style. These fabrics ravel and can be a sewer's nightmare, but they work well for this project. Some solid-colored fabrics become translucent where the adhesive is applied and the overlapping layers will show through. The finished vase has a ceramic look when finished with a gloss sealer.

You can create fabric mâché on any kind of plastic, wooden, or glass container (Fig. 10.2). Styrofoam packing is a fantastic form for a rectangular vase. Glue the two halves together and make sure the opening is the right size. Plastic and glass containers are suitable for fresh flowers because they can be filled with water. Salad dressing bottles have a graceful, but recognizable shape. Plastic maple syrup bottles are interesting because they have a

Fig. 10.2 Fabric mâché vases made by Kitty Wan and Tonny Smith of San Diego, California. Containers are glass, plastic, Styrofoam, cardboard, and plaster.

handle. If you decide to cut off the threaded section at the top of a plastic bottle, make a new opening by gluing a piece of heavy craft cord into a ring, then attach it to the bottle with a glue gun.

Minor changes can be made to the shape of the vase by applying several layers of 1"-wide (25mm) fabric strips. The cut edges will barely show and calico prints blend together as the strips overlap. Simple, bold prints are interesting but show the edges more than smaller prints. You may find that using 1" squares of fabric cut with pinking shears makes it easier to follow the contours of the container. This cut edge is more forgiving than one cut with regular scissors. For a variation, cut a heart shape with pinking shears in the center of a square. Apply it to the vase, exposing a contrasting fabric in the cut-out. The squares may also be applied with a slight overlap to give a patchwork effect when using assorted fabrics.

1 Keep a bowl of water nearby for quick cleanup. You might want to work with a glove on the hand you use for cutting to keep it unsticky because it seems you never have enough fabric strips cut. Cut 1"-wide (25mm) bias strips into 3" (76mm) sections.

2 Pour white craft glue into a dish and coat each strip on the wrong side, then apply it to the container. Layer pieces evenly. Use a paint brush to smooth the fabric and to apply more glue on the edges if needed.

3 Air or sun dry as the weather permits. Use a hair dryer to speed up the drying process.

4 The container doesn't need to be sealed; the glue will take care of that. When the vase is thoroughly dry, coat it with a sealant. A matte sealant will not be noticeable and will add strength to the construction. For a ceramic or glasslike finish, apply two coats of a clear acrylic medium, the base used for artist's acrylic paints.

PROJECT: PADDED AND COVERED CACHEPOT

Consider all the containers previously mentioned. Any of them can be covered with thermal interfacings or quilt batting (Fig. 10.3). The shape of the container can be changed by adding graduated layers of batting. Hot glue will secure a simple layer of padding or multiple layers to the container. If you have wrapped the padding over the top of the vase, then glue a piece of fabric to the inside that will come over the lip and finish about 2" (51mm) below the opening. This covered opening is only necessary when you want to pad the lip. The circular cover is gathered and cinched near the top of the vase. The techniques are for sewing machines and sergers.

MAKE YOUR PATTERN

Use a full sheet of newspaper to make a pattern for the cover. Draw two intersecting lines in the center and place the padded container

Fig. 10.3 Covered cachepots can be made from a large jar and a can.

at the intersection. Bring the pattern paper up to the top and pin it to the padded container. Hold it in place with a string or rubber band while you arrange the folds until the paper is evenly distributed around the container. Trim the paper to the desired length. Decide if you want a ruffled edge that is cut even, scalloped, or with points. Make allowances in the pattern for the ruffle length or for a casing if you want elastic in the top for a simple opening.

Remove the pattern and press flat. Make a final draft by drawing a perfect circle with a compass or by evenly spacing scallops on the edge. To draw a circle larger than a compass will allow, push a thumbtack in the center of the pattern and tie a string to it 5" (127mm) longer than the radius. Tie or tape the other end to a pencil and draw the cutting edge and gathering line. Use this method with a wash-out pen on the fabric to transfer dots for making the bartacks.

Hold the finished cover in place with a ribbon. You can make several covers for the same container and change them with the season or holiday. Imagine receiving a gift with such versatility! When making a cachepot with an assortment of covers, use a solid fabric to cover the padded opening. If you cinch the ribbon above the container's opening, the inside of the container won't be visible once the flowers are in place.

EDGE THE COVER

Chapter 3 offers many ways to edge flower petals that may be appropriate for the fabric cover for your vase. These include an assortment of sewing machine and serger stitched edges, sizzled edges, and painted edges. Ruffled or flat lace sewn on the edge makes a feminine cachepot cover.

GATHERING OPTIONS ON COVERS

The cover is held in place over the padded container by simply tying a ribbon around the top. If you would like the ribbon or cord held in place, here are some fun ways to make a casing. To determine the length of the drawstring that must pass through a casing, measure the circumference of the stitching line for the casing and add 10" (254mm). Tack the cord or ribbon in the middle of its length after inserting it into the casing to prevent it from pulling out (Fig. 10.4).

Use a zigzag wide enough to stitch over the gathering cord without sewing through it. Crochet cotton or a heavier cord makes a strong drawstring. Set your sewing machine for a long length. Draw a circle on the right side of the vase cover fabric with a washout pen. With an all-purpose foot, zigzag over the cord on this drawn line. Bring the stitching threads to the wrong side and knot (Fig. 10.5, top).

Another type of casing resembles mini belt loops for a 1/16" to 1/8" (3.2mm) ribbon (Fig. 10.5, middle). Draw a stitching line on the right side of the fabric cover. Set your sewing machine for a 4mm or wider zigzag. Lower

the feed dogs or set up for sewing on buttons by changing to 0 length. Stitch a bartack across the drawn line every 2" (51mm). Thread the end of a narrow ribbon through a blunt-tipped needle and pass through all the mini button loops. Consider using a variegated thread for the bartacks.

The flatlock setup on a serger makes an interesting casing (Fig. 10.5, bottom). You will need to draw a stitching line on the wrong side of the fabric cover. On most overlocks, using the right needle position will provide a stitch wide enough to make a casing for 1/8" (3.2mm) ribbon. Set a long stitch length.

You will serge on the wrong side of the fabric with the outer edge folded under on the stitching line. Overlap the last stitching by 1/2" (13mm) over the beginning stitching. By serging a flatlock on the fold, a ladder stitch will appear on the right side of the fabric when you pop it open after the sewing is done. Thread a narrow ribbon through a blunt-tipped needle and weave it over and under at least three stitches at a time, repeating a pattern. Serging thread that contrasts with the ribbon color creates an attractive pattern.

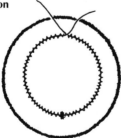

Fig. 10.4 Stitching a casing on the cachepot cover.

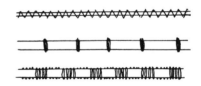

Fig. 10.5 (Top) Casing made by zigzagging over a cord. (Middle) Bartack casing for narrow ribbon. (Bottom) Flatlock casing for narrow ribbon.

PROJECT: CORDED BASKETS BY MACHINE

This basket is the kind of project that always garners the response, "You did that on your sewing machine?" This is a compliment in

disguise because the astonishment acknowledges that you are not only very skilled but also very clever. You will love being on the receiving end of this comment. Your response is "Of course I used my sewing machine. It just takes a simple setup."

The basket is made of a cotton clothesline cord wrapped with fabric strips (Fig. 10.6). Many successful baskets have been made using assorted craft ropes, printed bias tapes, and even precovered cords from fabric stores. If you are lucky, these items may be marked down because crafters haven't figured out enough ways to use them. After we discuss the basic construction, read on to learn about handles, edges, and lids, as well as ways to decorate the rope baskets. The baskets are surprisingly sturdy and most are machine-washable.

Smaller baskets hold coins or gadgets on dressers or desktops. Larger sizes are perfect for fruit bowls or tote bags. Sooner or later you will notice someone trying on your basket for a hat, a silly—but irresistible—thing to do. Baskets made by machine are definitely one of the fun ways to use your sewing machine.

Fig. 10.6 Corded baskets made by Debbie Casteel of Livermore, California, and Kitty Wan of San Diego.

All the materials to cover the cotton cord included here produce different effects. Make a small coaster or a hot pad from each kind of material so you can see the results before making an entire basket. I must warn you that these projects are so much fun that you may end up with a lot of baskets instead of just sample coasters. Consider using the following materials: printed bias tape, 1" (25mm) bias strips, 1" (25mm) strips cut on-grain, lace strips, decorative yarn, plaids, stripes, single knits, hand-painted or dyed fabric.

Machine Setup

Automatic stitch: three-step zigzag, serpentine, or wide zigzag with 3 length
Stitch length: average
Stitch width: wide
Feed dogs: up
Presser foot: all-purpose
Upper tension: normal
Lower tension: normal
Needle size: #90 (14)
Top thread: monofilament or poly-cotton
Bobbin thread: monofilament or poly-cotton

These three stitches are listed in the order of my preference, but any one will work. Baskets can be sewn with all-purpose sewing thread whose color blends into the fabric print, but using a clear thread in the bobbin will keep the stitching almost invisible when your basket is done.

CONSTRUCTION

1 Wrap the beginning end of the cord with a fabric strip (Fig. 10.7). Bend the end of the covered cord so you can sew it to itself in order to start the spiral. Sew in a clockwise direction. This spiral will become the bottom of the basket. While the work is still in the sewing machine, and with the needle down, wrap a few inches of the rope and continue stitching the coils together.

2 It is easier to work with strips less than a yard in length. When you reach the end of one strip, join the next strip by overlapping 1" (25mm) and continue wrapping the cord.

3 When you have stitched long enough to make the bottom of the basket, it is time to start bringing up the sides by forcing the bottom to roll on its side to the left of the sewing machine (Fig. 10.8). If you don't bring the

sides up high enough as you stitch, you will end up with a platter instead of a basket.

4 When you are ready to finish the basket, cut the end of the cord to a smooth taper. Continue to wrap the taper, cut the fabric, and stitch the coils to secure and finish (Fig. 10.9).

Fig. 10.7 Start the basket by wrapping a tapered cord with bias fabric strip until you have made the bottom of a basket.

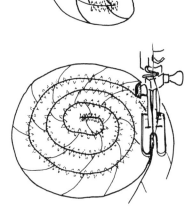

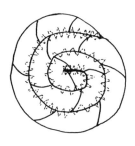

Fig. 10.9 End the basket on the lip by cutting and wrapping the cord to a tapered end and machine stitching to secure.

VARIATIONS

After making your first basket, you will understand more clearly how the shape can change depending on whether you increase or decrease the circumference of each layer of rope. You can control this in two ways. If you stretch the cord as you stitch it in place, the basket walls will gradually pull to the inside and the opening will decrease. By concentrating on rolling the basket toward or away from the machine, you will determine the eventual shape.

In addition to using an assortment of fabrics, you can wrap a strand of yarn around the rope core with ½" (13mm) intervals. If you concentrate on even spacing between the wraps, striped pattern magically spirals from the center bottom of the basket. Without any effort, the wraps align themselves. This method is the fastest way to decorate the basket as you sew, without using fabric strips.

If you would like to try using a lighter-weight craft or macramé rope, braid, twist, or chain a few strands together to make the rope more substantial. Some of these ropes may be too lightweight for baskets. Whether you use a lightweight cord or multiple cords, see Chap-

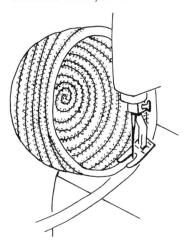

Fig. 10.8 Form the basket sides by turning the bottom on its side while you continue to add more rows.

ter 3 for ways to stiffen the finished basket if you want a firmer shape.

HANDLES AND EDGES

While you are sewing your basket, decide if you want to include side handles or a decorative edge along the top. These are easy ways to accent a plain basket. To make a handle on opposite sides of the basket, make a loop with the cord but don't sew it to the previous row. A large wooden macramé bead in this loop makes an attractive side handle; a wooden thread spool works, too. On the other side of the loop or bead, continue stitching over the cord, connecting the current and previous rows (Fig. 10.10A).

A scalloped edge is done the same way as the handles, except there are many loops all around the top edge. When the basket is finished, roll the edge down. For a heavier edge, remove the work from the sewing machine and weave additional cords in and out of these loops (Fig. 10.10B).

Before you cut the cord, remove the basket

Fig. 10.10 (A) Large bead or spool over the cord for side handles. (B) Scallops undulate on the basket's edge. (C) Carrying handle made from the cord of the basket. (D) Cord knob on the top of a lid.

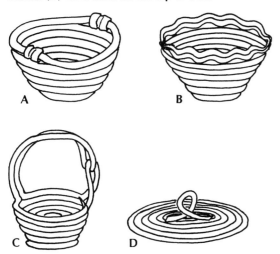

from your sewing machine and pull up the sides to see how the basket would look with a carrying handle that goes over the top like an Easter basket. Clearly, this style is not appropriate for every basket you make, but it is a fun variation. Determine how much cord you will need to make the handle before you start sewing that part. The handles continue from the cord on the basket and may be formed into a chain, twisted, or simply two cords stitched side by side. The weakest part is where the handle joins the basket, and this is why the handle isn't made separately and then attached. The shorter the handle, the better it will hold itself in place (Fig. 10.10C).

LIDS

The lid can either lie on top of the basket or it can cup over the top edge of the basket. This is almost like making a second basket, but here you will bring the sides up for only a few rows. A knob or loop of cord glued on the top is optional. Place it inconspicuously among the fabric flowers that decorate the cover (Fig. 10.10D).

SHAPING UP

It seems that all too often the first attempt at making a basket by machine is an underestimated success. If you manage to sew all the rows together without gaps and the sides are brought up, you have a winner! Most baskets can be touched up with additional stitching where two rows weren't connected. If you didn't bring up the sides of the basket, you may have instead a nice hot pad or coaster. If the sides rise only a little, then you have cleverly made a plate!

Let's get serious about shaping this creation into a basket. It probably has a rounded bottom and you need to make it sit flat. Place the basket on the table and force it down to give it an even, flat bottom. Next, shape the sides and top opening by pushing in or out. Turn the basket inside out; you might like the shape better. If the cord produces a flimsy basket or you really got carried away and made a gigantic urn, spray the finished piece with fabric stiffener. (See Chapter 3 for as-sorted stiffeners.) Spraying will shoot a fine mist between all the rows and coat the cording evenly. Most stiffeners dry clear, but you may want to try your choice of stiffener on a coaster-size sample to see if the finished look harmonizes with the fabric.

PROJECT: STIFFENED FABRIC SACK

I first thought about making a fabric sack to hold flowers when I fell in love with a $50 ceramic vase that looked just like a miniature crumpled brown paper bag. Its high price prevented me from making such an extravagant purchase. But if I ever see them on sale . . . So, like many of my unique sewing projects, these stiffened fabric sacks were created to satisfy my need for something I couldn't have. Sometimes I don't get the exact results I'm aiming for, but the adventure is fun.

If you use a lightweight tan fabric, the sack will look like it is made from paper. Gauze fabric has lots of character after it is stiffened. Cotton twills and burlap have good body and appear to be sturdy (Fig. 10.11). Both Aleene's Fabric Stiffener and clear acrylic medium are easy to use and stiffen the fabrics to a wonderful crisp finish. A second coat of acrylic medium will give the fabric a glossy, porcelain finish. Use it, too, to glue sequins to the fabric when painted on.

CONSTRUCTION

The basic fabric sack is made from a single layer of fabric that is soaked with fabric stiffener after the sewing is complete. You can add personalized labels while sewing the sack. After the sack has been stiffened, trim the top edge with pinking shears to complete the look of authenticity. The ribbon or cord tied around the finished sack appears to hold everything in place.

Figure 10.12 gives the dimensions for your paper pattern. The small fabric sack will finish about 7-½" (19cm) tall before it is shaped.

1 Cut out your fabric using your paper pattern. Place the fabric on top of the paper pattern and fold and press one crease at a time, matching the paper pattern. Press all the four outer creases and one inner and one bottom crease. (There are two inner creases, but one is formed by sewing the side seam.)

2 Attach any label or patch to the sack while the fabric is flat.

3 Sew the ¼" (6.4mm) side seam. Only a straight stitch is needed since the stiffened sack will not ravel. Finish the seam by cutting with pinking shears for the paper sack look.

Fig. 10.11 Stiffened sacks made from assorted fabrics decorated with paint, glitter, and a tie by Kitty Wan of San Diego.

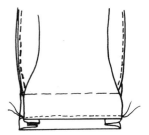

| 11" (28cm) | | |

outer crease · outer crease · inner crease · outer crease · outer crease

8½" (21.5cm)

¼" (6.4mm)

¾" (19mm)

3 ¾"   3 ¾"   3 ¾"   3 ¾"

¾" (19mm)

¼" (6.4mm)

Fig. 10.12 Measurements and fold lines for stiffened sack.

4 Topstitch the four outer creases and one inner crease from the top edge of the sack to the bottom horizontal crease (Fig. 10.13). The side seam does not need to be topstitched.

5 Turn the sack inside out and fold all six of the vertical side creases opposite of how they were sewn. Pin and sew a ¼" (6.4mm) bottom seam through all the layers (Fig. 10.14).

6 Turn the sack right side out and topstitch the bottom horizontal crease.

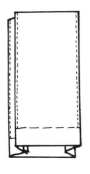

Fig. 10.13 Sew the side seam, then topstitch the four outer creases and one inner crease that go from the top of the sack to the bottom crease.

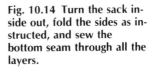

Fig. 10.14 Turn the sack inside out, fold the sides as instructed, and sew the bottom seam through all the layers.

SHAPING AND DRYING

Choose among the choices of fabric stiffeners in Chapter 3. Those appropriate for fabric sacks include Aleene's Fabric Stiffener, the sugar starch recipe, clear acrylic medium, and any craft or floral spray sealant.

1 If you use Aleene's Fabric Stiffener or acrylic medium, pour it into a resealable plastic bag. Aleene's may be diluted with white glue or a little water for a thinner consistency.

2 Place the fabric sack in the plastic bag and zip closed after squeezing out the air.

Squeeze the bag to force the fabric to become completely soaked with the liquid. As you remove the sack, squeeze the excess liquid into the plastic bag. If all goes well, you will have a minimal sticky mess.

3 Snip a corner on the bottom of the plastic bag and squeeze the remaining fabric stiffener back into the bottle for future use.

4 The fabric will dry in about an hour on a warm day. Use a hair dryer if you want to speed up the process. The smaller sack can be hung upside down to dry until tacky, then set it on its base once you have stuffed and shaped it. For a perfectly flat bottom, put an aluminum-foil-covered piece of cardboard on the bottom. If you want to use the sack to hold fresh flowers, put a spice or baby food jar inside while it is drying and surround it with crinkled foil so the shape will conform when the ribbon is tied. Use an empty paper towel roll to hold the shape if you don't have a small jar or if you intend the sack for fabric flowers. Set it to dry on a nonstick cookie sheet or on a piece of foil. Wrinkle the fabric to add character to the sack. This is no time for perfection.

5 When the fabric sack has dried thoroughly, cut the top edge with pinking shears for an authentic paper-bag look. Make sure to sign your name and date on the bag with a fine-tipped permanent pen. This often-forgotten special touch makes your creation unique and personalized from you, the designer. A dedication can be added when the occasion arises.

11

Patterns

The patterns included throughout the book for each project can be used for appliqués, machine embroidery, or three-dimensional flowers, or with a little imagination, can be used interchangeably for any technique. Pressed fresh and silk flowers also provide good sources of inspiration for patterns. There is nothing like making a pattern from the real thing.

Trace the outline of the flowers, then enlarge the drawings at different percentages on a photocopying machine. If you want an extremely large pattern, use the largest percentage, then enlarge the enlarged copy. If your anticipated copy is too big for the paper, cut it into sections and enlarge each section. Tape the final pieces together like a puzzle. This method worked for me when I converted a drawing into a 4' × 5' banner. Usually I make a grid over artwork to enlarge it by drawing it to scale, but that time the original design was composed of hundreds of dots and I needed to enlarge them accurately.

An opaque projector will allow you to project nearly unlimited enlarged sizes of images from paper to a wall. You will have to draw the projection on paper with the bright light at your back. If you don't mind the hassle, schools usually have these scarcely used projectors and may let you borrow one. Some projects are worth the effort of obtaining this cumbersome equipment and finding a work space and wall to accommodate the task.

This chapter contains more patterns and basic ways to vary each of them. Consider a sin-

gle petal shape and how many ways you can change it to resemble petals for other flowers (Fig. 11.1) or use a single layer of petals or several layers of petals to create your own fantasy flowers. When you need several petals, cut a strip of fabric with the petal shape repeated across the length (Fig. 11.2). This technique is used to make daisies, sunflowers, cornflowers, carnations, and chrysanthemums.

Apply the idea of changing petal sizes or

Fig. 11.1 Altering a single petal to make other simple shapes.

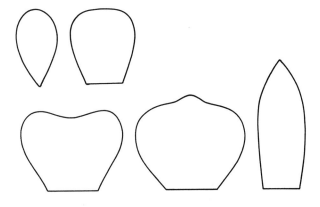

Fig. 11.2 Changing a single petal into a strip of petals and repeating the pattern for easy construction.

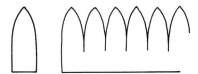

using multiple layers for an assortment of flowers. A single layer of rose petals will look like a poppy. By enlarging and making minor changes to the same style of petal, you will make a magnolia. Layers of daisy petals can be stacked to make a chrysanthemum. Flowers will change dramatically when the same pattern is used to make a wired or stuffed petal. More changes are possible when you cut the fabric on-grain or on the bias from woven or knits. The same ideas for altering the shapes of petals also apply to leaves.

The following patterns are 50% of actual size.

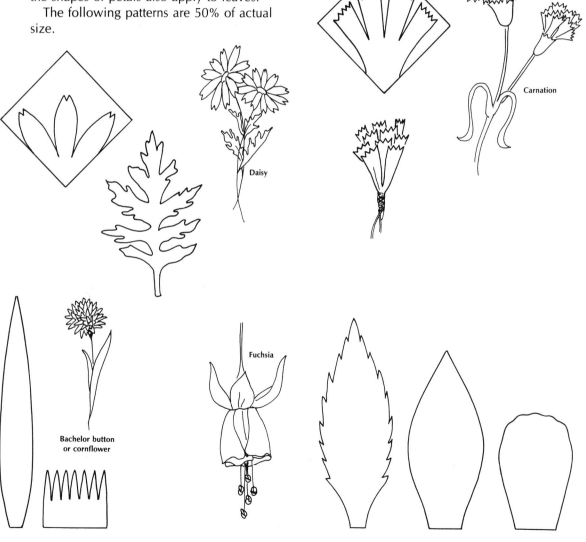

Carnation

Daisy

Bachelor button
or cornflower

Fuchsia

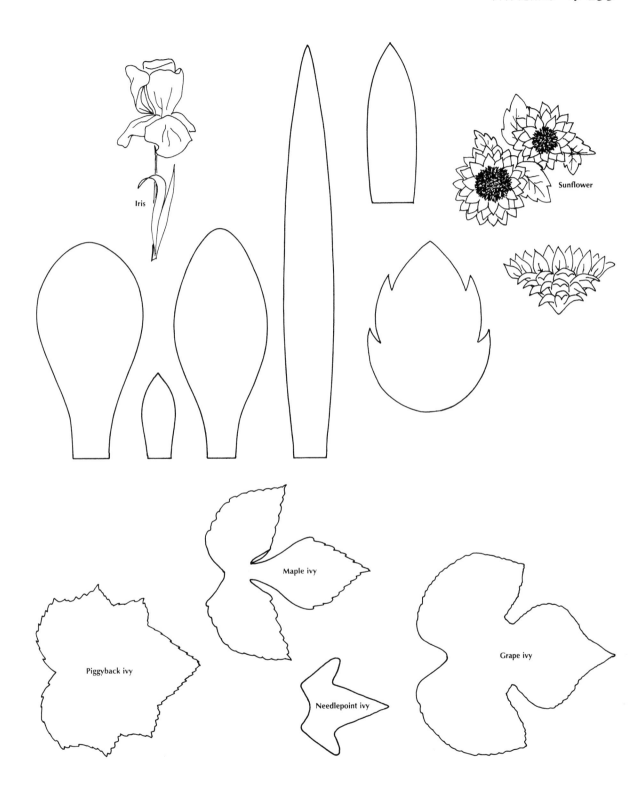

Iris

Sunflower

Maple ivy

Piggyback ivy

Needlepoint ivy

Grape ivy

Supply Sources

Beads and Jewelry Findings

The Crafty Critter
P.O. Box 16124
Duluth, MN 55816
(218) 624-7041
Beads, books, patterns for beading and appliqué by sewing machine.

Fire Mountain Gems
28195 Redwood Highway
Cave Junction, OR 97523
(800) 423-2319
Findings, tools, gemstone beads.

Lights

Balloon-Lite Co.
1195-A Linda Vista Drive
San Marcos, CA 92069
(619) 744-7297
Assorted balloon lighting systems.

Darice Inc.
21160 Drake Road
Strongsville, OH 44136
(800) 321-1494
Assorted light and musical light buttons, floral and fashion light sets.

Fiber Optics
Virgie Fisher
P.O. Box 214502
Sacramento, CA 95821
(916) 624-7310
Fiber-optic instruction manual and supplies.

Flora-Lite Co.
P.O. Box 4119
Clearwater, FL 34618
(813) 443-0369
Assorted floral and fashion lights.

Machine-Embroidery Supplies/Mail Order

These sources have extensive stock, and all are unique in their selection. Many of them have classes and seminars with nationally known machine artists. The items listed are ones that have been used in the projects and may be hard to find in local stores.

Aardvark Adventures
P.O. Box 2449
Livermore, CA 94551
(510) 443-ANTS
Mizuhiki, stabilizers, large buttons to cover, tassel earring kits, thread, transfer pens. Publisher of the catalogue ''Aardvark Territorial Enterprise.'' Send $2.00 for sample issue.

Clotilde Inc.
1909 S.W. First Avenue
Fort Lauderdale, FL 33315
(800) 772-2891
Stabilizers, Stuff-It tool, transfer methods, No-Stick Teflon sheet, Dried Floral Spray, lots of notions to make sewing easier.

Creative Stitches
P.O. Box 89
Bountiful, UT 84011
(800) 748-5144
Stabilizers, transfer methods.

Nancy's Notions
P.O. Box 683
Beaver Dam, WI 53916
(800) 833-0690
Stabilizers, transfer methods, notions.

Sew-Art International
P.O. Box 550
Bountiful, UT 84011
(800) 231-2787
Stabilizers, transfer methods.

Sewing Emporium
1079 3rd Avenue
Chula Vista, CA 91910
(619) 420-3490
Presser feet, accessories, scalloping shears.

Speed-Stitch, Inc.
3113-D Broadpoint Drive
Harbor Heights, FL 33983
(800) 874-4115
Stabilizers, transfer methods, many books from the Bibliography, Ultrasuede appliqué patterns.

Treadleart
25834-I Narbonne Ave.
Lomita, CA 90717
(800) 327-4222
Stabilizers, transfer methods, Ultrasuede appliqué
patterns, books, publishes *Treadleart* magazine.

Specialty Sewing Machine Presser Feet

Clotilde Inc.
1909 S.W. First Avenue
Fort Lauderdale, FL 33315
(800) 772-2891

Creative Feet
21704 Devonshire St., Suite 347
Chatsworth, CA 91311
(800) 776-6938

The Crowning Touch, Inc.
2410 Glory C Road
Medford, OR 97501
(503) 772-8430

Nancy's Notions, Ltd.
P.O. Box 683
Beaver Dam, WI 53916
(800) 833-0690

Sewing Emporium
1079 3rd Avenue
Chula Vista, CA 91910
(619) 420-3490

Threads

MACHINE EMBROIDERY
Assorted Threads

Madeira U.S.A.
56 Primrose Drive
O'Shea Industrial Park
Laconia, NH 03246

Rainbow Threads
803 S. Groveton Avenue
Glendora, CA 91740
(818) 335-9647

Robison-Anton Textile Co.
175 Bergen Blvd.
Fairview, NJ 07022

Brazilian embroidery rayons

Edmar Co.
P.O. Box 55
Camarillo, CA 93011
(805) 484-2306

DMC 100% cotton, #30 and #50

The DMC Corporation
107 Trumbull Street
Elizabeth, NJ 07206

Dual-Duty Plus Extra-Fine, cotton-wrapped polyester

J&P Coats/Coats & Clark
P.O. Box 6044
Norwalk, CT 06852

Iris 100% rayon

Art Sales
4801 W. Jefferson
Los Angeles, CA 90016

Iris 100% silk—*see* Zwicky

Mettler Metrosene machine-embroidery cotton 60/2

Swiss-Metrosene, Inc.
7780 Quincy Street
Willowbrook, IL 60521

Natesh 100% rayon

Aardvark Adventures
P.O. Box 2449
Livermore, CA 94551
(510) 443-2687

Renaissance 30% wool/70% acrylic and other threads

Sew-Art International
P.O. Box 550
Bountiful, UT 84011
(800) 231-2787

Sulky 100% rayon #30 and #40

Speed-Stitch, Inc.
3113-D Broadpoint Drive
Harbor Heights, FL 33983
(800) 874-4115

Zwicky 100% cotton #30/2

White Sewing Machine Co.
11750 Berea Road
Cleveland, OH 44111

METALLICS
Blending filaments, braids, and ribbon threads

Kreinik Mfg. Co., Inc.
9199 Reisterstown Rd., Suite 209B
Owings Mills, MD 21117
(800) 537-2166

Troy Thread & Textile Corp.
2300 W. Diversey Ave.
Chicago, IL 60647

YLI Corporation
45 West 300 North
Provo, UT 84601

Ultrasuede Scraps and Supplies

Jewell Box Treasures
4501 Kratzville Road
Evansville, IN 47710
(812) 424-1610
Hibiscus and Krinkled appliqué patterns.

Libby's Creations
103 Ross Lane
Vicksburg, MS 39180
Dimensional appliqué patterns and books.

Mary Jo's Cloth Shop
Gaston Mall
401 Cox Road
Gastonia, NC 28054
(800) MARY JOS
Ultrasuede yardage at discounted prices. 1/16 yd. minimum cut.

Nor-Mar Fabrics and Gifts
1327 Main Street
Napa, CA 94559
(707) 253-8577
Send sample of colors you need so they can match as closely as possible. Prices vary according to the size of the scrap.

The Sewing Arts, Inc.
390 Hudson Street
Denver, CO 80220
(303) 321-8037
Dimensional flower patterns for Facile and Ultrasuede by Shirley Smith.

Ultra Delight
Rt. 1 Box 117
Wheeler, TX 79096
(806) 375-2257
Appliqué and unique patterns, iron-on rhinestones, *Learning and Using Your Ruffler.*

UltraMouse Ltd.
3433 Bennington Ct.
Bloomfield Hills, MI 48301
$2.00 catalogue, scraps, rhinestones/setters, patterns for appliqués and gifts.

UltraScraps
P.O. Box 98 SW-2
Farmington, UT 84025
(801) 451-6361
Send $1.00 for catalogue only. Prices vary according to the size of the scrap.

Other Supplies

Ad-Tech
3 Merrill Industrial Drive
Hampton, NH 03842
(800) GLUE-GUN
Magic Melt Glitter Sticks, low-temperature glue guns, glue pads.

Advantage Products
P.O. Box 2358
Shingle Springs, CA 95682
(916) 644-3400
Tip-Pen metal applicators and extension caps for fine lines when using squeeze bottles.

Cherry Tree Toys, Inc.
P.O. Box 369
Belmont, OH 43718
(800) 848-4363
Wooden parts, kits, tools (candle cups for calyxes).

Clover Needlecraft, Inc.
1007 E. Dominguez St. Suite L
Carson, CA 90746
(310) 516-7846
Wavy-edged fabric shears.

The Crowning Touch, Inc.
2410 Glory C Road, Dept. P
Medford, OR 97501
(503) 772-8430
Fasturn tools, Fastube presser foot, adapter, patterns, and jewelry findings for turned tubes.

Designs By Bentwood, Inc.
P.O. Box 1676
170 Big Star Drive
Thomasville, GA 31799
(912) 226-1223
Bentwood boxes, wooden slatted baskets, and trays.

Palmer/Pletsch
P.O. Box 12046
Portland, OR 97212
(800) 728-3784
Perfect Sew wash-away liquid stabilizer.

Sakura of America
30780 San Clemente Street
Hayward, CA 94544
(800) 776-6257
Pigma Micron pens and Fashion Craft Markers.

Yasutomo & Co.
490 Eccles Avenue
South San Francisco, CA 94080
(800) 262-6454
Mizuhiki (Japanese paper cord).

Bibliography

Baker, Carolynn. ''Twin-Needle Fill-In,'' vol. 13, nos. 4 and 5, Jan./Feb. and Mar./Apr. 1991. Available from *Treadleart*, 25834-I Narbonne Ave., Lomita, CA 90717.

Bennet, dj. *Machine Embroidery with Style*. Seattle: Madrona Publishers, 1980.

Black, Leota. *Learning and Using Your Ruffler*. Available from Ultra Delight, Route 1, Box 117, Wheeler, TX 79096.

Body Blueprints. *The Art and Craft of Ribbon Work*. Available from Body Blueprints, 1 Lower Via Casitas, Greenbrae, CA 94904.

Clucas, Joy. *The New Machine Embroidery*. Devon, England: David and Charles Publishers, 1987.

Dodson, Jackie. *Know Your Sewing Machine*. Radnor, PA: Chilton Book Company, 1988.

Fanning, Robbie, and Tony Fanning. *The Complete Book of Machine Embroidery*. Radnor, PA: Chilton Book Company, 1986.

Fettner, Ann Tucker. *Potpourri, Incense, and Other Fragrant Concoctions*. New York: Workman Publishing Company, 1977.

Freitas, Maria A. *Brazilian Embroidery Book I, II, and III*. Camarillo, CA: Edmar Co., 1991.

Holt, Verna. *Simple—ly Elegant Machine Stitchery*. Twentynine Palms, CA: Homestead Publishers and Distributors, 1988.

Jeffery, Vera. *Handmade Flowers*. Santa Monica, CA: Exeter Books, 1980.

Joynes, Heather. *Creative Ribbon Embroidery*. Kangaroo Press, 1989.

Kling, Candace. ''Candace Kling's Ribbon Fantasies,'' *Treasures in Needlework*, spring 1992, pp. 34–37. (For a copy of this issue, send $4 to Craft Ways Publications, 4118 Lakeside Drive, Richmond, CA 94806.)

McGehee, Linda F. *Texture with Textiles*. Available from 106 E. Kings Hwy., Ste 205, Shreveport, LA 71104.

Montague, Rosie. *Brazilian Three-Dimensional Embroidery*. New York: Dover Publications, 1983.

Montano, Judith. *Crazy Quilt Odyssey/Adventures in Victorian Needlework*. Martinez, CA: C & T Publishing, 1991.

Osmus, Mary Ray. *Machine Embroidery Stitches and Techniques Instruction Workbook*. (1990). Available from 506 Baylor Court, Benicia, CA 1990.

Plummer, Beverly. *Fragrance/How to Make Natural Soaps, Scents, and Sundries*. New York: Atheneum, 1975.

Schultz, Tecla Miceli. *Greeting Cards by the Dozen*. (1984). Available from 120 East Birch, Brea, CA 92621.

Shaw, George Russell. *Knots Useful and Ornamental*. New York: Bonanza Books 1933.

Singer Sewing Machine Company. *Instructions for Art Embroidery and Lace Work*. 1911.

Tower, Libby. *Elegant Way to Appliqué, vols. 1 and 2* (1984). Available from Libby's Creations, 103 Ross Lane, Vicksburg, MS 39180.

Index